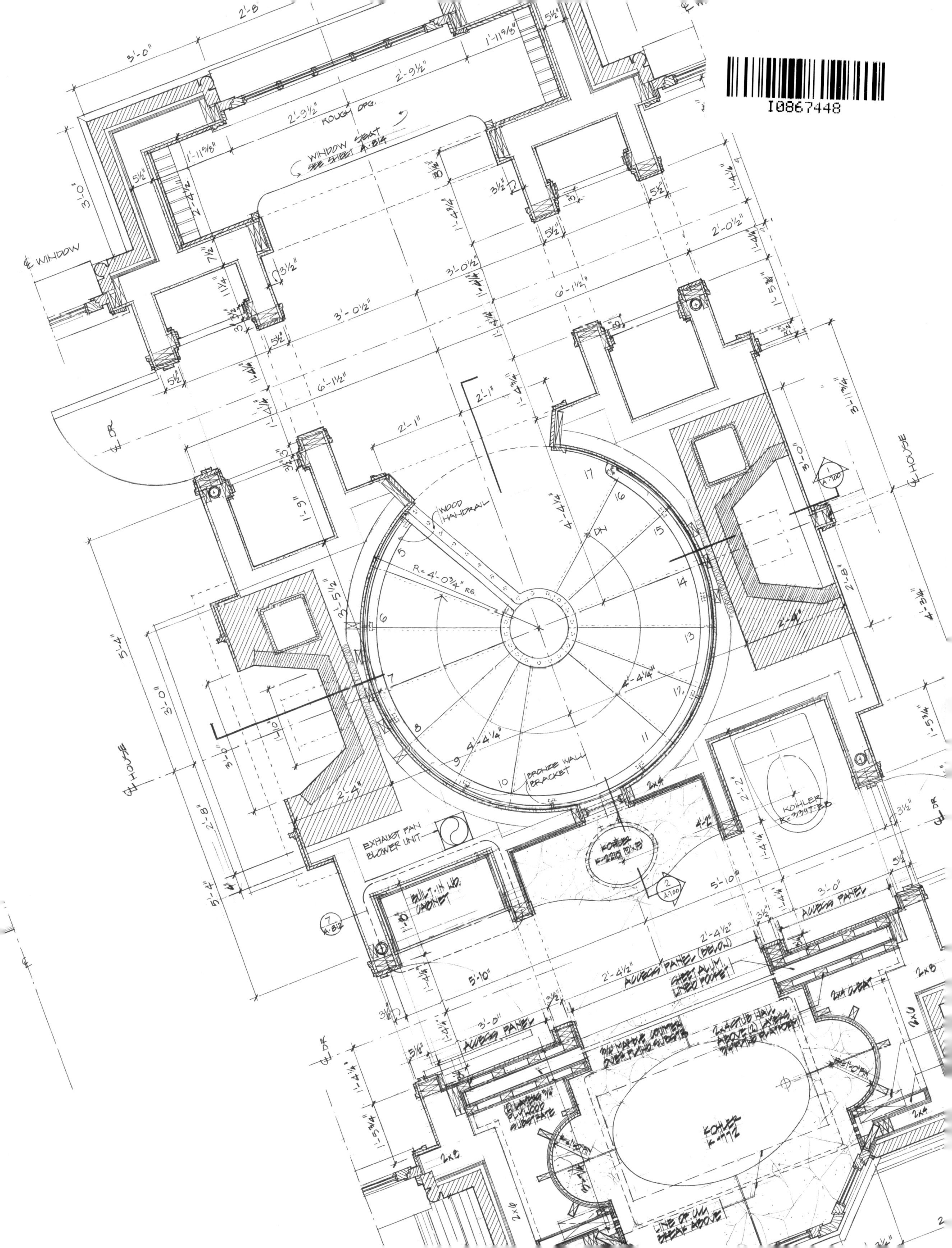
WINDOW SEAT
SEE SHEET A-814
ROUGH OPG.
℄ WINDOW
℄ DR
℄ HOUSE
WOOD HANDRAIL
R=4'-0¾" RG.
BRONZE WALL BRACKET
EXHAUST FAN BLOWER UNIT
BUILT-IN WD. CABINET
KOHLER
ACCESS PANEL
ACCESS PANEL (BELOW)
SHEET ALUM. LINED POCKET
2x4 CLEAT
2x8
2x6
2x4
2x10
KOHLER K-772
I0867448

OLIVER COPE ARCHITECT

CITY · COUNTRY · SEA

Foreword by Alisa and Dan Doctoroff
Written by Nicolas Kemper
Introduction by Clive Aslet

TRIGLYPH BOOKS

THE HAMPTONS

CONTENTS

Dedicated to our clients.
Without them, our work would not be possible.

FOREWORD

Alisa and Dan Doctoroff

Some thirty years ago, as a young couple contemplating a small renovation of an apartment to make it more family friendly, we were introduced to Oliver Cope. We should really say "re-introduced", because we quickly discovered that this Oliver Cope was the same one who had been our college classmate. Our lives since that time have included several major renovation and construction projects, including a townhouse, a beach house and another apartment. And, fortunately, each project has included Oliver.

We and our family have been delighted with the outcomes, with the graciousness, beauty, and functionality of the spaces Oliver and his team designed for us. Each project had different design challenges and, at the different stages of life at which we found ourselves, different living requirements. In each case, though, we have taken great pleasure in the process, in the creative collaboration of designing our homes together with Oliver - and other talented design professionals - for living, working, gathering, celebrating, playing, and relaxing.

From the start we trusted Oliver's exceptional instincts and talents for thinking about space, the people who would occupy it, and how the space and people could flourish together over time. When we thought we were looking for one more room in an apartment for our growing family, we ended up with a townhouse originally built in 1896 and in bad repair. Would we really have taken on the gutting of an entire house without him? He gave us the confidence to imagine, to think it through step by step, to consider all the options. How did we want to live? Formal or informal? Where would we spend our time? Where did we want to invest the most money? He listened, he suggested, he puzzled out solutions. He guided us in the selection of a superb contractor, Steve Mark, who has ended up being part of our long-term team, too. Collaboration with decorator Victoria Hagan yielded a house that was elegant and timeless, all the details beautifully resolved. There were grand spaces for entertaining and for holiday celebrations. And lots of space for our three children, ages three to eight, to be children and for our family to hang out together and with friends.

As clients and architect, we have also had the opportunity to grow together. Our beach house in Quogue is a case in point. Unlike the townhouse, there was no building envelope to work within.

We had no preconceived notion of the style we wanted for the ocean-front property that we had purchased. There was no house we could point to as a model, whether among the houses Oliver had designed previously or beyond. But we did know that we wanted to take advantage of the magnificent views and, as city dwellers, to feel and experience the outside even when inside. Oliver was only too happy to explore with us and to stretch his vocabulary.

An important piece of the design work was siting the house on the land and contemplating not only its relationship to the ocean, but also to the neighboring homes. Oliver brought in a talented landscape architect, Ed Hollander, to help us with that vision. He then managed the town approval process as if he had served in government for decades and handled the delicate negotiations with our neighbors with the tact of a longtime diplomat.

For the beach project, we added the fabulous Eve Robinson to the mix as decorator. The result is an L-shaped, shingled house, composed of several adjoining boxes with sloping roofs. A combination of traditional beach materials – shingles – and modern glass openings and shapes. Importantly, the public rooms, pool and deck sit up on the second floor, with the L opening to the vista of dunes and ocean beyond. We only wish we could spend more time in its glorious space!

The apartment on Central Park West offered another type of challenge. We were attracted to the space by the views and light that came through its large windows, but the apartment was built at a time when kitchens were unseen in the back and spaces were cut up into a series of small rooms. With Oliver's help we reimagined the traditional configuration, even eliminating a static, formal dining room. The light from the front bleeds directly through the entire living area into the open kitchen. In addition, the new design suits the informal way we live most of the time, but enables formal entertaining when desired.

City, Country, Sea illuminates Oliver's inspired work across each of these settings. We have experienced the best of both city and sea with him. If there is a "country" project in our future, we know the architect to call.

INTRODUCTION

by Clive Aslet

I first met Oliver Cope when we were touring some of Sir Edwin Lutyens' country houses in England. Lutyens is one of Oliver's heroes from the architectural Golden Age of the early 20th century. Oliver's knowledge and enthusiasm made me want to discover more about his own practice, so I went to New York. There I found him at work with his long-time colleagues, Olivia Rowan and Rita Marks in the office of Oliver Cope Architect, near Madison Square Park. This is a versatile team who work fluently across several styles, always focused on the work before them rather than the media attention it might bring. Hence this book. We agreed that it was time their exceptional homes were shared with a wider public.

Craft is important for this firm. It stands in a tradition of Harrie T. Lindeberg, Delano & Aldrich and the other great domestic architects of the early twentieth century, whose houses were nothing if not beautifully built. The work of these firms had a British counterpart in that of Sir Edwin Lutyens, whose native genius for three-dimensional form was conjoined to an exuberant love of hand-crafted materials. These architects, born within 10 years of each other, from 1869 (Lutyens) to 1879 (Lindeberg), took an aesthetic delight in the subtle variations of finish that resulted from the use of craftsmen rather than machines. In the spirit of William Morris, they believed in the sanctity of place: their houses are so well adapted to the landscapes in which they sit that they almost seem to have grown out of the soil. OCA shares these values. They can be seen on every page of this book.

There is the play of light on the staircase of a beach house at Quogue, or the elegance with which they restored, in the original idiom, an Upper East Side townhouse by Walker & Gillette defaced by a Depression era storefront. Photographs alone cannot capture the subtlety of the fireplace in the big room of a house in Locust Valley, New York: a small deflection in the otherwise plain block of Cippolino marble to break the surface. Or the discretion of the moldings in a New York apartment. You are, perhaps, barely aware of them, but subliminally they contribute to the comfortable feeling that every detail has been thought about and resolved. The style may be Colonial, French Renaissance, Shingle or Contemporary, depending on the preference of the client. But style is never everything. It is complemented by a sense of domestic completeness. Once you are inside an OCA home, it will feel calm, well-ordered, right.

Rightness results, in part, from the sense of resolution in the architecture; there are no loose ends to tie up. However challenging the geometry of a butterfly plan or a complicated staircase, the ceilings above will always be elegantly shaped. Architectural ideas create not only beauty but problems; Oliver and his team are meticulous about seeing they are solved. The finished work is like a Rubik's cube, with all the colors on each of the faces lining up. It creates a sense of satisfaction in the viewer, even if he or she does not know precisely how it is done, or perhaps does not actually notice. Some things are deliberately hidden from sight; for example, services that may be tucked away behind grilles concealed in a baseboard or the soffit of an arch. This is architecture at its most complex – for residential structures demand far more time than office or institutional buildings. Details matter.

Homes grow out of their plans. The rooms of an OCA residence unfold a sequence of contrasting spaces, sometimes dramatic, always adapted to the way clients want to live now. There is a comparison here with Lutyens, whose houses are a theatre of surprises. First impressions may deliberately deceive. So it is with the façade of an OCA house on Long Island. The inward-curving entrance façade – a reference to Lutyens' Greywalls at Gullane - looks quite modest, with pediments that break the roofline in a French manner. And yet this unfolds as a house of some splendor. It is also, though you would not know it as you approach, right on the water. You open the front door and opposite are large French doors framing a living picture of shore and sea.

In a Jacobean-style country house (p.68-83) at Old Westbury, the irregular site, falling on one side, was turned into an opportunity: it allowed the architects to place the big card room half a dozen steps lower than the rest of the house, giving it greater height and a degree of flamboyance it would not otherwise have had. Coziness, when wanted in this room, is to be found in the inglenook; a house should always have an inglenook if it can. This is a project that has grown to reflect life on the property; as well as the main house there is now a large garage for the machines necessary to maintain the private golf course, as well as an apartment for the groundskeeper, a pool pavilion, a tennis pavilion, a pump house and a guest house.

Making sense of an old property – teasing a fully functional plan out of a sequence of spaces created for a different era – is something of an OCA specialty. Even a home by the great Delano & Aldrich at Old Westbury may be capable of improvement, given that it was built in the 1930s. Two subordinate side wings have been remodeled, providing a music room with a silvered vault (the vault was created by raising the ceiling into the loft space) in the one; next to it is a glamorous bar. In the other wing, a double-height kitchen has been made out of a warren of old service rooms. No doubt the family who commissioned this house almost a century ago would hardly ever have gone into the kitchen, certainly not to eat or cook; and the staff would have lived out of sight. Conditions change and houses should change with them. The home has been brought into an era in which kitchens are now the hub of domestic life and staff do not habitually wear white gloves. This work has been done in a spirit of respect to the original building. An existing circular vestibule on one side of the house is echoed in a slightly larger circular space on the other. The outside of this handsome mansion remains virtually untouched.

Then, materials. Oliver and his fellow directors, Olivia Rowan and Rita Marks, delight in the stuff of which their work is made, be it Indiana limestone or cedar shingle, book-matched elm burl veneer or mahogany paneling. You can feel this joy in the nougat of randomly laid stone, tawny brown and blue-grey, in a house on Long Island (masonry that can be compared to Lindeberg's in the Harry F. Knight mansion of around 1925). A lodge in the Adirondacks celebrates the rustic in wood and boulder. Hand-made bricks, with a sandy finish, create the walls of the Jacobean-style house at Old Westbury; they are complemented by the mottled red of the roof tiles, again hand-made, and the creamy grey of Indiana limestone. There are numerous carved ornaments, richly detailed chimneys and lovingly conceived turrets. Upstairs in a house on Centre Island, overlooking Oyster Bay, a window is set in an expertly cut limestone niche, whose stones diminish in width as they curve towards the center. OCA knows where to find the best craftsmen – stonemasons from the National Cathedral in Washington, D.C., for example. Work of the highest quality can be seen throughout the book.

This is a firm that rejoices in building soundly; contractors often praise the highly informed working drawings that it supplies for their thoroughness. But it also believes in pushing boundaries. Dramatic overhangs, large expanses of glass that appear to contravene hurricane codes, constructional techniques that combine steel and wood to unite function with beauty – all may initially be questioned by engineers but agreed upon once the solution has been worked out by the architects and put before them. "I'm asking people to do things that are a little out there," says Oliver. "But to get what I want, we have to fully engage on how it needs to be done and then communicate it in the drawings. I am stubborn about getting what I want." This is where those comprehensive drawings come in again. OCA houses are not built by rote; often, the architects need to explain precisely how to achieve their effects.

Ingenuity is a tool of their trade. In the early days of the firm, Oliver was asked to remodel a boat house as a guest house on Centre Island, on Oyster Bay. Eagerly he set to work and obtained a building permit within six weeks. This led to a request that he should design a new house on the same site because the clients wanted to be free to pursue a more ambitious project. He explained that the zoning codes would not permit it. And yet, as though by a sleight of hand, he succeeded in devising a scheme that allowed him to remove the roof and put concrete columns through the brick walls; a concrete beam was then poured across the top of the walls and from column to column allowing a second floor and roof to be constructed. After the second floor and roof were complete, the old first-floor brick walls were removed, leaving the concrete columns supporting the house above and awaiting first floor walls to be installed. The original building had disappeared, and yet at no point could it have been said not to be there. Success here so impressed the client that he was given the job of replacing the big house on the property; it was something of a coup.

Like Lutyens' practice, OCA has benefitted from a close association with landscape architects, such as Peter Cummin and Edmund Hollander; its country places sit well in their natural surroundings. For example, the house and stables in Locust Valley, (p.54-67) are set among a gracefully rolling greensward, in which the horses appear as the crowning feature, overlooked at a slight distance from the house; and yet before work started, the hillside had been an impenetrable thicket. One difference with the work of Lutyens, however, is in the relationship with decorators. Lutyens never had much time for them (his houses could be austere). Not so Oliver Cope. The practice strives to work creatively with the other professions involved in the making of a home. The result is a harmony between all the parts and players.

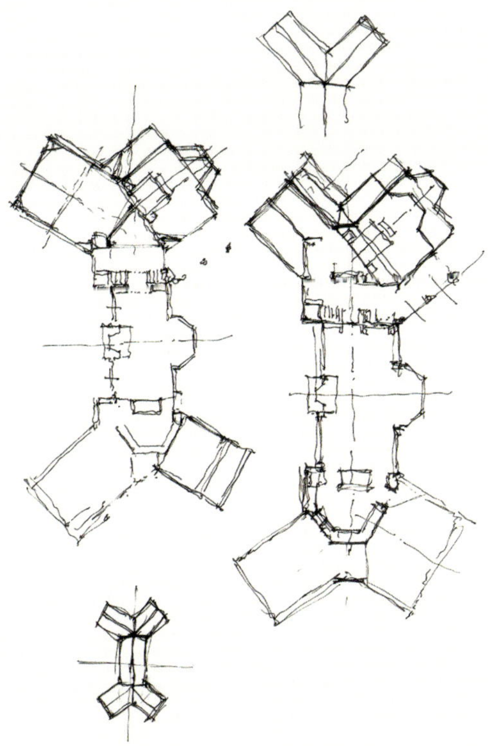

(Process) Every home begins as a sketch *(top left)*. In office iterations and charettes ripen and resolve initial ideas – on the bottom left, Jairo Castro draws in the office's library. Continued attention *(top right)* ensures the best outcome, as evident on the bottom right in the stone carved details of our Country Estate home *(pg.68)*.

THE PRINCIPALS

The three principals of Oliver Cope Architect are Oliver Cope, Olivia Rowan and Rita Marks.

As a boy, Oliver loved making things. He grew up in New England, where his father, a lawyer, organized family projects. "Weekend and summer life revolved around erecting a new garage, building stone walls, fixing plumbing. This," he says, "is what we did for fun. It's what I still do for fun." At his country home on Long Island, down time from the office has recently been spent hand-crafting a French workbench after the designs of André Roubo, an 18th century furniture maker and author. This delight in the practical side of construction explains not only the high level of craftsmanship in the architecture but also why it works so well. Solving the conundrums of practical life and making a space deliver as much as it can to the client are a source of much pleasure to the team.

Architecture is in Oliver Cope's DNA. A great-grandfather from Philadelphia was Walter Cope; a Quaker, he founded Cope & Stewardson with his childhood friend, John Stewardson, in 1885. Cope and Stewardson had a rapid success with their collegiate Gothic style architecture for Bryn Mawr College, the University of Pennsylvania and Princeton, but both principals died young, Cope from a cerebral hemorrhage, Stewardson from falling through ice on the Schuylkill River while skating. Both a son, Thomas P. Cope, and a daughter, Elizabeth Cope Aub, were trained as architects; Elizabeth, one of few women to graduate from MIT in architecture in the 1920s, went on to have a business making architectural models.

The first job that exposed Oliver to the arts of building came in 1974, when he was seventeen. His grandparents' house was being renovated by local contractors who also built solar homes. At the height of the energy crisis, solar power caught Oliver's imagination; he got a summer job as a carpenter's helper at $1.90 an hour. "I had a great time. I learned a lot. One of the partners couldn't understand why I was going to Harvard and didn't stay working for them; he had gone to Harvard himself so he was making a wry point." But to Harvard Oliver went, studying biology. The lure of building was still strong – in his junior year, he took a semester out; he had spent his tuition money on buying a wreck of a brick town house to renovate. After finishing the work, he rented out the rooms and mortgaged the house, returning to college.

By now, Oliver was also studying architectural history, in a class taught by Neil Levine. This gave him a more sophisticated understanding of the Shingle Style architecture amid which he had grown up, as well as introducing him to giants such as Henry Hobson Richardson, whose 'Cyclopean' Ames Gate Lodge continues to inspire. Harvard boasts Le Corbusier's only building in the United States, the Carpenter Center for the Visual Arts, which Oliver also admired. It was there, in a life drawing class, that he met a model maker, working for a big architectural firm; he gave Oliver some part time work. Skill with models also brought him to the attention of the architects at Cambridge Seven, founded by Ivan and Peter Chermayeff and others. He went to work there as an office boy, using his practical skills to help upgrade their office. In his spare time, he added a solar greenhouse to his parents' home.

The Graduate School of Design at Harvard beckoned. "I was fortunate that at the time Modernism was out of favor at Harvard. My teachers were interested in the use of precedent in design and the making of spaces, whether urban or architectural. A lot of attention was paid to the section as well as the plan of buildings.

It was about creating spaces, both within buildings and with buildings themselves, rather than simply objects." A classmate introduced Oliver to the work of Lutyens; it was a revelation. He soon acquired a number of what became well-thumbed books on the architect. One of the GSD teachers was Bruno Pfister, then a senior associate of Kallmann McKinnell & Wood; his lectures focused on the way that design intent should inform construction and detail. This approach resonated with Oliver, who was already building a house in Vermont for his brother and some of his brother's friends (it was, Oliver remembers, a distraction from his thesis). He became Pfister's teaching assistant.

On Pfister's recommendation the University of Cincinnati hired Oliver as an assistant professor after his graduation. He was already building homes in Rhode Island and Maine for old family friends so the University agreed to fly him to Ohio for two days each week. He remembers organizing slide decks on architectural history on the airplane. When they offered to make him full time, he demurred: business was picking up, and he would rather build. Oliver's passion for history, however, continued unabated, still reflected in the well-stocked shelves in the office library and the piles of books at his desk.

Oliver's early work quickly met with acclaim. A client described their Rhode Island Shingle to *House Beautiful* as a place where "some spaces soar and some are for snuggling." *Home Magazine* named a cottage on Martha's Vineyard designed by Oliver on a shoestring as the "Best Little House," enjoying how it "echoes local architecture" while managing to "stretch tradition to gain spaciousness." When Oliver was thirty, he left New England for New York, to be with his future wife, Hillary. The first article in *House Beautiful* led to a commission for a large house on an island off the Connecticut coast for a client with whom he has continued to work ever since. His career was launched. Once the practice was underway, clients came in a steady stream, generally by recommendation. The rest is the story of this book, with its dazzling succession of homes in city, country and by the sea.

~

Olivia Rowan comes from Ireland, having studied at University College Dublin in the early 1980s. UCD's School of Architecture at the time espoused a wide range of design thought. Olivia was taught by professors who advocated creating rooms in plan and were considered neo-traditionalists, like O'Donnell + Tuomey (RIBA Gold medal winners in 2015) and by the 2020 Pritzker laureates Yvonne Farrell and Shelley McNamara (Olivia's thesis tutor) of Grafton Architects, who taught open plan design influenced by the International Style. During a year out, Olivia worked for the Greater London Council, designing public housing; she also traveled widely around the UK, Ireland and Europe, visiting the architecture she was studying. She graduated in 1985.

This was a slow time for the Irish economy and it was hard for fledgling architects to find jobs. Olivia's classmates went to London, Paris, New York and Sydney. She made her destination New York, working for the small, inventive firm of Vandeburg and Lasky before joining the office of Robert A.M. Stern, famous for its high-end residential commissions and rediscovery of the Shingle Style. This chimed with the work of Lutyens, C.F.A. Voysey and other Arts and Crafts architects which she had studied in Dublin. She moved to OCA in 1990 to help work on the boat house on Centre Island already described. She says that she "loves the challenge of working with the clients' dreams and dealing with the uniqueness of each site, the zoning restrictions and the intricacies of creating a structure with all the services hidden from view." She continues to travel extensively to research architecture and building techniques.

There were only four people in the office when Olivia joined it, as opposed to the nineteen people there now. Olivia and Oliver developed a method of working which has continued to this day, working up early ideas on tracing paper and passing them back and forth for the other's comments. Olivia enjoys this phase of work; volumes are beginning to coalesce, plans starting to take shape, roof lines emerging. She has always drawn by hand, sketching three-dimensionally, throughout the design process of the many large houses on which she has worked at OCA. "Later it is very exciting to see that design being realized in bricks and mortar." The process is more fluid when the house is in the Shingle Style with its bays, towers and porches: Colonial is "a little less forgiving, with its more formal rules." The spectacular Contemporary beach house at Quogue, a place of big windows and wooden walkways amid the dunes, partly powered by geothermal and solar energy, was "a really wonderful design opportunity."

OCA is fortunate in its clients. "We get to design a house all the way through. We enjoy designing every last piece, including the millwork, moldings, mantelpieces and occasionally the light fixtures." And every job is different. "We try not to repeat details. Every house is individually designed." Over the years, "projects seem to have enlarged," reflecting the increased amounts of personal space amid which people want to live. Formal dining rooms may be less in vogue than family kitchens, recreation rooms, media rooms and gyms but all will have to be detailed and built to the same exacting standards; "the craftsmen we work with are incredible."

~

Rita Marks is always sketching. This suited her for a career with OCA, which she first joined in the early 1990s. Her studies began in 1974 at the Rhode Island School of Design during the energy crisis; there was no work in Providence, even for her professors who had to rely on teaching to see them through a dark period. So in 1976 she moved to New York and finished her education, graduating in 1979 at the Pratt School of Architecture while spending all the time that she could working in architects' offices. At the end of the course, she found herself placed in an office next to a man who had studied at the École des Beaux-Arts in Paris; "he was making drawings in ink and wash. That was art." A new world of possibilities opened up. Afterwards, she began her career designing commercial projects, but found them unsatisfying. There was an element of sameness about the commissions. She then spent some time working for decorators. When she chanced upon OCA as a firm that designed houses, she immediately responded to the variety it offered.

One of her first projects at OCA was for a shingle-clad house in Pennsylvania, with dormer windows in the deep roof. Today she has become something of a specialist in town houses. She has been the lead architect on five. Town house projects are ruled by "enormous constraints" that do not usually apply outside of New York City; the Landmarks Preservation Commission may have a say, along with organizations such as the Friends of the Upper East Side. There is an innate conservatism in some communities. Finding a way through the forest of legal protection and public opinion requires patience and skill; and similar problem-solving skills are needed to resolve the architectural complexities. "I love the puzzle," says Rita. "Everything has to be packed in vertically. There is all this swirl of information, so many things to consider; you have to clarify and define what is important."

The result is an intellectual challenge, whose rigor corresponds to the formal architectural language often used by OCA. "Maybe I'm the sort of person who likes ground rules," she says.

Rita also designs fast. Schemes flow from her pencil in an unending stream. "I run out as many as I have time for. There are so many ideas that they have to be whittled down; Oliver is an excellent editor." Meanwhile, she maintains an archive of magazine clippings as a resource for future use. Many of these clippings are devoted to craftsmen who may come in handy one day. "You never know when you'll need a metal screen thirty feet high. There's an artist in St Louis who will do one."

CLIENTS

OCA clients come from many worlds: finance, medicine, real estate, the law. One thing that unites many of them is the willingness with which they return to the firm or recommend it to other family members. One client has commissioned, over time, a country house, a beach house, an apartment and a town house. There are webs of connection between brothers, children, cousins and friends of clients who, having seen and experienced an OCA house, then go to the firm for one like it. This is how the practice has grown over the years. OCA has sought little press coverage, published no manifesto, does not seek a profile through teaching work, debating on panels, or taking a position on new public works; nor does it often participate in competitions. Instead word is passed from friend to friend, relative to relative, neighbor to neighbor.

This is a matter of considerable pride for the firm. What better evidence that these architects understand their craft?

OLIVER COPE

Left, Rita Marks,
Center, Olivia Rowan,
Right, Oliver Cope

Oliver Cope received an A.B. from Harvard College in 1980, a Master of Architecture from Harvard Graduate School of Design in 1985 and was a Visiting Assistant Professor of Architecture at the University of Cincinnati. His early career experience was at the firms of Beyer Blinder Belle Architects & Planners in New York City and David P. Handlin Associates in Cambridge, Massachusetts before establishing the firm of Oliver Cope Architect in New York City in 1988.

Oliver Cope is licensed in the states of New York, Connecticut, Maryland, Florida, Massachusetts and Pennsylvania and is a member of several professional and architectural organizations including The Institute of Classical Architecture and Art and the American Institute of Architects.

OLIVIA ROWAN

Olivia Rowan's love for good design started early with time spent traveling throughout Europe. She received her degree in Architecture from University College Dublin, Ireland, in 1985. After working in London, she moved to New York City and gained experience in high-end residential work while in the employment of Robert A.M. Stern.

In 1990 she joined Oliver Cope Architect and has since designed and run many of the firm's major projects. Her experience encompasses all variety of projects from New York City apartments to estates on Long Island and in Connecticut.

Ms. Rowan's work with Oliver Cope Architect has appeared in many publications including *Architectural Digest*, *Ocean Homes*, *Private Air Magazine* and *The Wall Street Journal*. She has won multiple awards for her work from the American Institute of Architects, and from Brick in Architecture. Ms. Rowan is a registered Architect in the state of New York and a member of the American Institute of Architects.

RITA MARKS

Rita Marks began with Oliver Cope Architect in 1994. As Senior Designer and project manager on many of the firm's townhouse and apartment renovations, Ms. Marks has a wealth of experience with New York City residential projects and understands the challenges and opportunities city projects offer. Recent projects include a townhouse renovation in the Landmark District of Carnegie Hill, renovations to Upper East Side townhouses on 69th and 70th Streets and a Gracie Square duplex renovation. In addition, she has managed teams as designer for residences in East Hampton, New York and Old Westbury, New York.

Before her tenure at Oliver Cope Architect, she contributed to high-end residential projects for Sandra Nunnerly, Eric Smith, Richard Sammons and Juan Pablo Molyneux.

Ms. Marks received her Bachelor of Architecture from Pratt Institute in 1979, starting at Rhode Island School of Design. She is a registered Architect in the State of New York and a member of the American Institute of Architects.

COUNTRY

STONE HOUSE

OLD WESTBURY
NEW YORK

Our firm is no stranger to making plans work within the constraint of a given boundary. This case, however, was a bit extreme. A misbegotten start left the owner with a twenty-five-foot hole in the ground, along with the permits for a sprawling footprint and volume, when he approached our firm for help. The client had one clear reference, an admiration for the Tudor houses of the garden city outside Philadelphia, Chestnut Hill. Tudor is a style associated with the very emergence of the home as we understand it.

Tudor is named for the Tudor monarchs Henry VII, Henry VIII, Edward VI, Mary, and Elizabeth I. Their reigns saw a time of sufficient peace that a standalone dwelling no longer required fortification –could even venture some windows. The peace heralded a broad wave of prosperity, and the middle classes began expanding what had been rudimentary cottages to become real homes, with the halls, libraries, and even discrete bedrooms that had previously been the domain of only a few. The expansions were opportunistic, sometimes just one room, and the material would shift from one to the next. Yet a keen sense of proportion, skilled craftsmanship, and attention to detail made for homes large but intimate, diverse but coherent. It was little surprise then that as home construction surged in both England and America at the end of the nineteenth century, architects ranging from Lutyens to Frank Lloyd Wright to Grosvenor Atterbury would adopt and revive this language to meet the needs of an increasingly prosperous country. The gold standard in this Tudor-boom were the one hundred sixty fieldstone Cotswold Tudor houses of developer Dr. George Woodward in Chestnut Hill, almost all designed by just three architects with such coherence that they established a local vernacular.

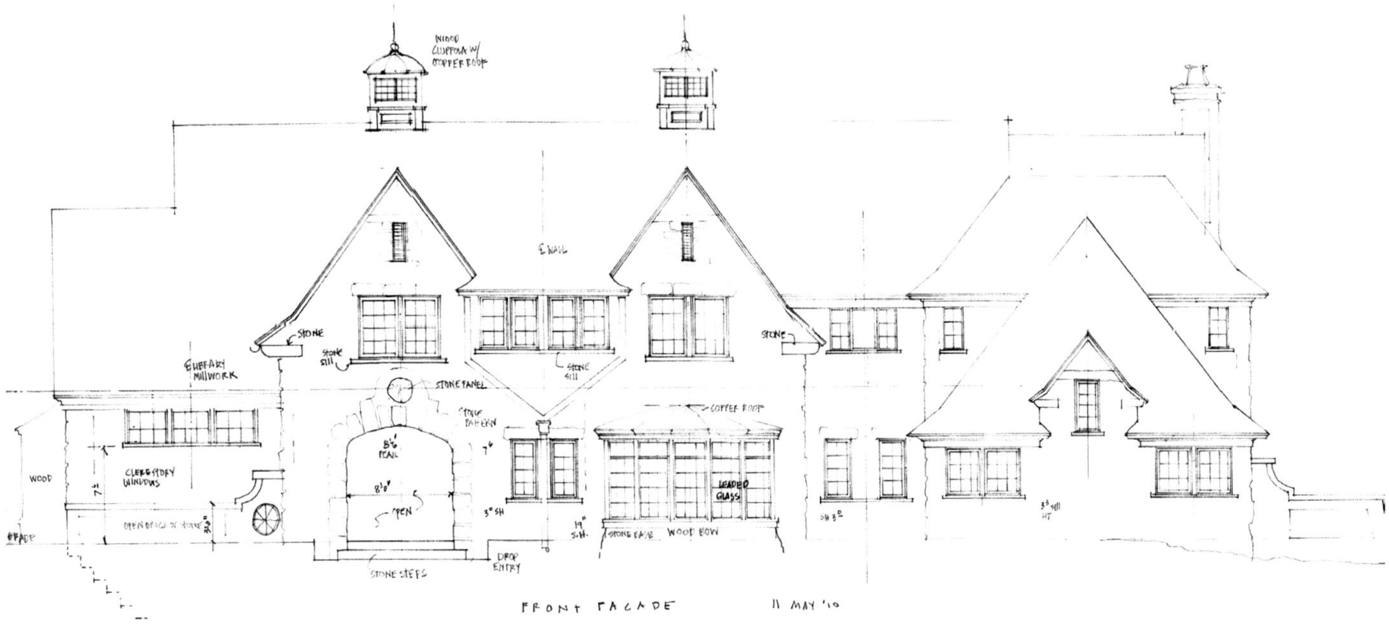

But back to our hole in the ground. To find additional inspiration, we turned to a local legend from that same period, the architect Harrie T. Lindeberg. Working around New York, his houses merged the informality and flexibility of Tudor with what was at that time the other dominant strain in American residential design, the axial elegance of Classicism. The family was large and had diverse and modern needs, ranging from a spacious and light filled kitchen with a connected breakfast and family room, to a dining room to accommodate weekly dinners for the extended family, to a room particularly important for our client, a peaceful library. We made each of these rooms unique and suited to its purpose. While keeping its proportions humane, to accommodate these rooms, we let the house ramble on the exterior. By preserving all the existing trees and using the same slate roofs and random rubble fieldstone as the Chestnut Hill houses, we made the house appear as though it had always been there. On the interior, we established clear axes and adjacencies between the different rooms – we forged relationships.

A second-floor hallway runs from a corkscrew staircase and mezzanine in the library to the main staircase. That staircase pins the dining room to the central first floor hall. The central hall, library, and living room all rotate off this entrance hall. Distinct from the formal rooms, the kitchen, family room and breakfast room share an open plan that extends – through windows and doors – to the yard, garden, and pool beyond. Finally, a craftsmanship and shared vocabulary, that ranges from moldings to the trim, ties the entire house together. The doors are all the same, which we feel simply makes a house feel good.

Craftsmanship comes to a high point in the library. We worked with Hardwick Post and Beam to create the timber vaulted space. They found large reclaimed oak timbers with the depth necessary for the arc cut in the tall principal bents that define the space. Collaboration between architect, millworker and timber framer celebrates the oak and its strengths, rustic and refined.

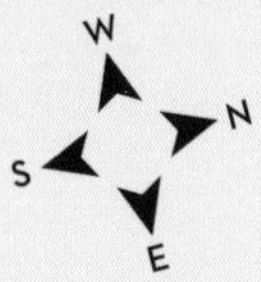

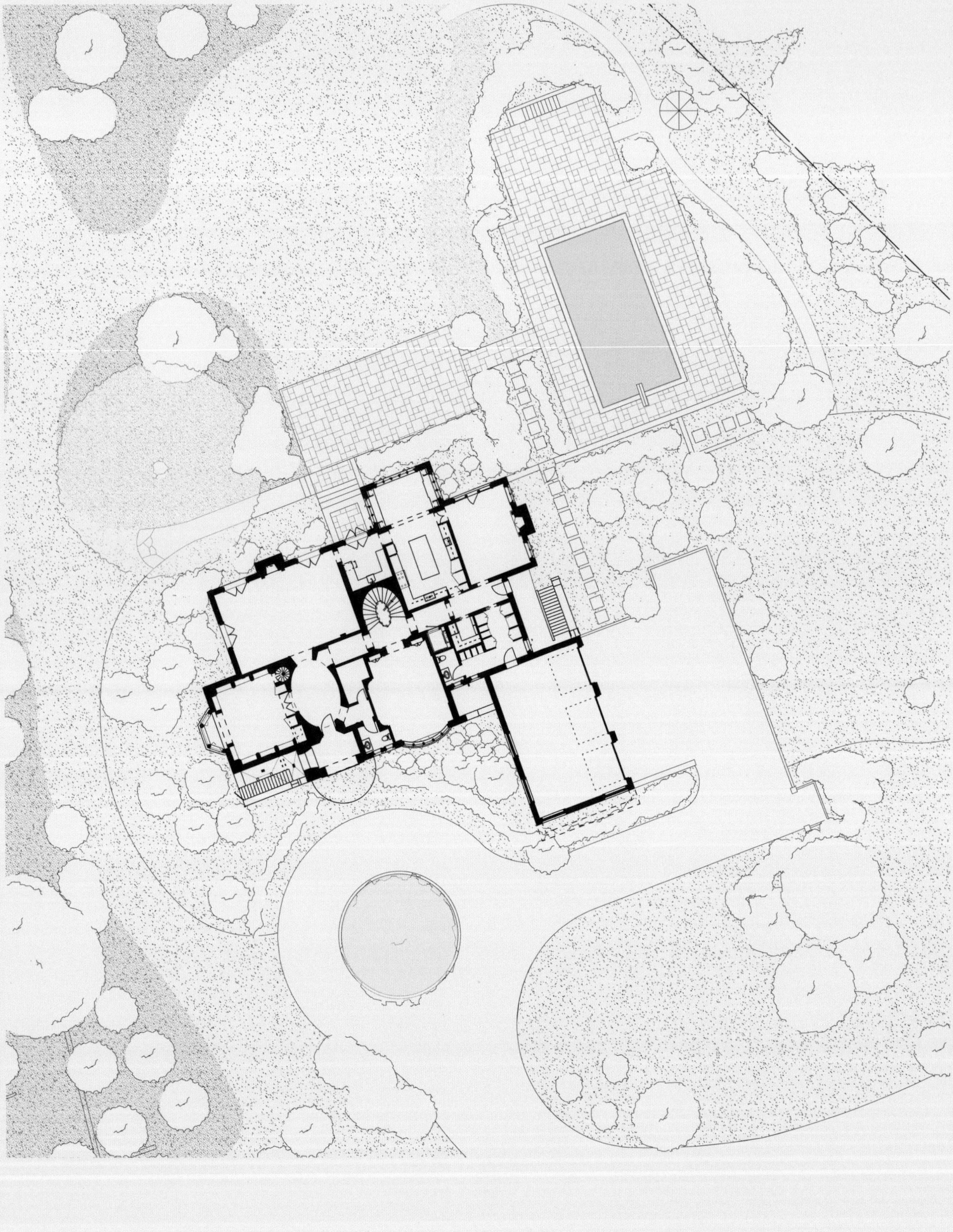

SITE PLAN

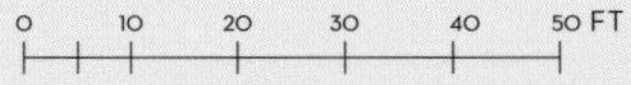

FIRST FLOOR

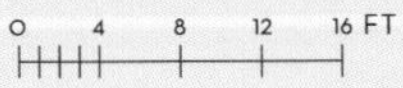

1. COVERED ENTRY
2. ENTRY FOYER
3. LIBRARY
4. LIVING ROOM
5. STAIR HALL
6. BAR/BUTLER'S PANTRY
7. KITCHEN
8. BREAKFAST ROOM
9. DEN
10. PANTRY
11. MUD HALL
12. GARAGE
13. DINING ROOM
14. CLOAK ROOM

–

Spread 28-29, &
Page 31 (Exterior Shots),
The random rubble fieldstone exterior makes the home appear as though it has always been there.

Page 33 (Elliptical Stair),
The main stair runs from the lower level to the third floor.

–

Opposite, (Bay Window),
A view of the entry arch and the dining room bay window.

This Page, (Font Door),
The front door, made from painted mahogany, has bronze strapping and leaded bullseye glass.

–

(Library), For the library, we had to find reclaimed oak timbers with the depth necessary for the arc cut in the tall principal bents that define the space. Ellie Cullman's interior decoration complements the warmth of the wood and welcomes you in.

–

(Upstairs Hall),
The second-floor hallway runs to a spiral stair in the library.

–

This Page & Opposite, (Kitchen & Breakfast Room),
The kitchen opens, through a simplified Tudor arch, to the breakfast room, which does double duty as a homework spot.

–

Project Drawing, Rita Marks
Project Photography, Durston Saylor

ADIRONDACK HOUSE

NORTH ELBA
NEW YORK

To be "forever kept as wild and forest lands" is the mandate Article VII, Section 7 of New York's Constitution set forth in 1894 for the state's forest preserve, Adirondack Park. Today its six point one million acres hold the origin of the Hudson River and span more than ten thousand lakes and thirty thousand miles of rivers and streams. The preserve protects these vital watersheds that are essential to the economy and operation of New York's cities. At the same time, it protects a vital spiritual counterpoint to the city. The untouched mountains and old growth forests are there to offer sport, retreat, and arguably sanity for the downstream inhabitants in their concrete forests.

This retreat to nature requires homes in harmony with their environment. At the end of the 19th century, William West Durant developed just such a home in the Adirondack Camp. Seeking to lure tourists onto his father's railroad and into his family's vast land holdings, William West Durant employed local craftsmen to build houses and hotels – invariably called 'Camps' – in a method that drew upon and even augmented their surrounding beauty. Over the course of thirty years, he and his craftsmen established a truly unique American vernacular tradition that endures to this day.

We built upon that tradition when a family came to our office with a site perched above the town of Lake Placid. The site was set deeply in the forest, on a slope offering a 180-degree view of the High Peaks and directly facing across the valley to the Wright, Algonquin and Iroquois Peaks. The family asked for a home at one with this setting. After testing a series of different approaches, a simple massing held the most promise. Echoing the mountains that surround it, the roof has foothills and peaks. The home is open to nature. Indeed, the deck and porch are nearly half the first floor. Windows framing the sweeping view line the kitchen,

the living room, and the study. The bedrooms above hug the same view. The parents report that, in the summer, they almost exclusively use the sleeping porch, with its screens on three sides.

Our family planned on coming here all year round, and an Adirondack winter is no joke. To make the interiors feel cozy, the walls are finished in warm-toned natural woods. Fireplaces anchor the living room, a study, the screened in porch, and the kitchen. A spacious mudroom has room for boots, skis, and lots of, well, mud.

That same winter made construction challenging. There was nothing here before we arrived, just forest. An access road was built, the building site was cleared and leveled. A custom roof truss system, fabricated off-site, made it possible to close in the house quickly and before the snows arrived.

Durant's Adirondack vernacular comes out through the details. To house the stairs, we drew upon the vocabulary of a forest fire tower. In the rooms, roughhewn logs and branches become beams and balustrades. Crooked members are left crooked. Bark was left put. Lights hang on simple chains or rest in birds' nests of twigs. Our points of reference were not all local. Durant did not in fact step foot in the Adirondacks until he was twenty-seven – while his father built a railroad empire, he had his son raised in Europe. There he visited the Alps and studied at Twickenham in England. Both the Swiss Chalet and the budding English Romantic and Picturesque movements played roles therefore in the origins of the Adirondack Camp. In the same way, we looked to examples of Eliel Saarinen's early houses and their play of vertical against horizontal.

The result is a home that is both ready for the summer, while warm and safe against the winter, a project built in a challenging context, that is nevertheless in tune to that context.

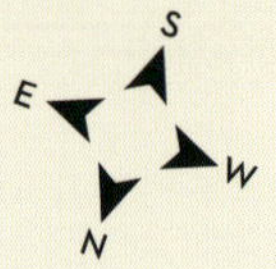

FIRST FLOOR

1. ENTRY
2. HALL
3. LIVING ROOM
4. KITCHEN
5. STUDY
6 GUEST BEDROOM
7. STAIR HALL
8. PANTRY
9. OFFICE
10. MUDROOM
11. SPORTS CLOSET/LAUNDRY
12. BACK ENTRY
13. SCREENED PORCH
14. GARAGE
15. PORCH
16. DECK

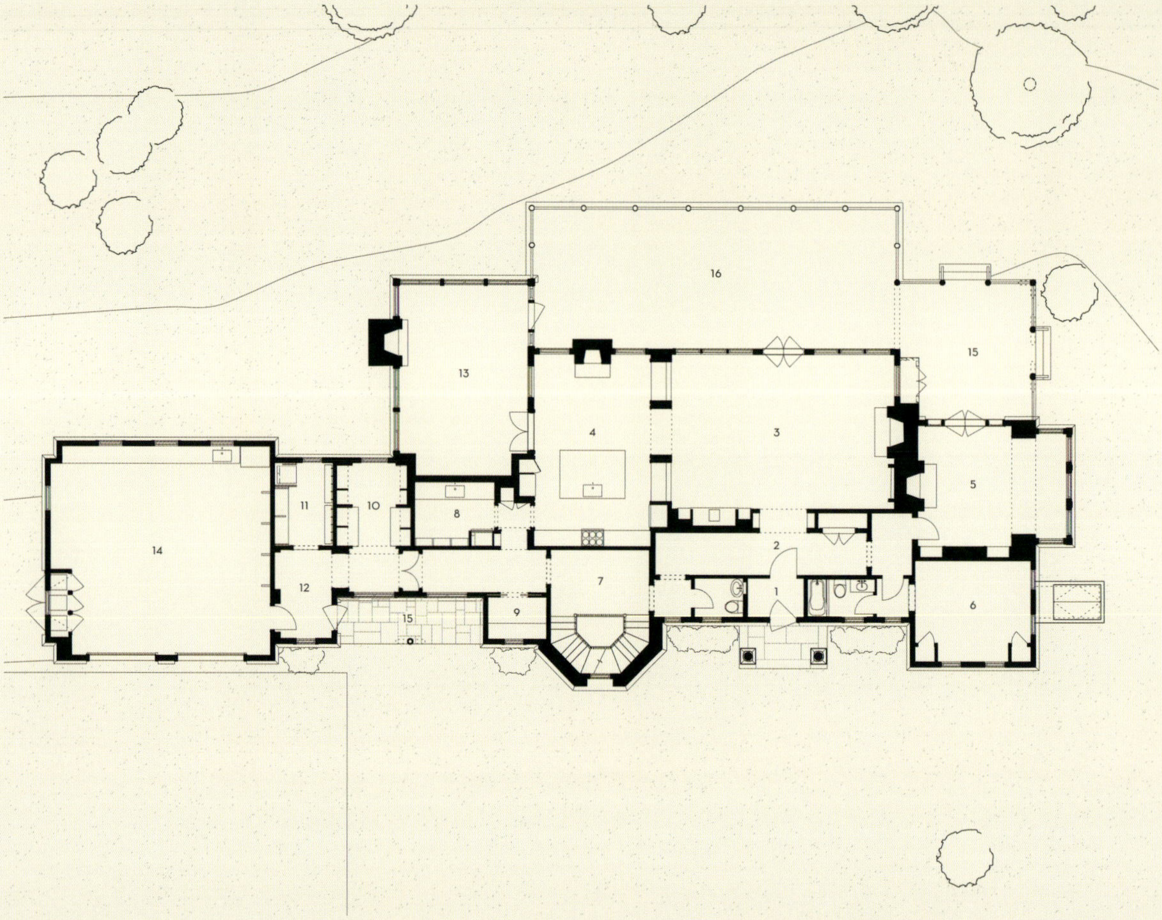

SECOND FLOOR

1. STAIR HALL
2. BEDROOM
3. MASTER BEDROOM
4. DRESSING ROOM
5. SLEEPING PORCH
6. MASTER BATHROOM
7. LAUNDRY
8. HALL
9. BUNK ROOM
10. PLAYROOM

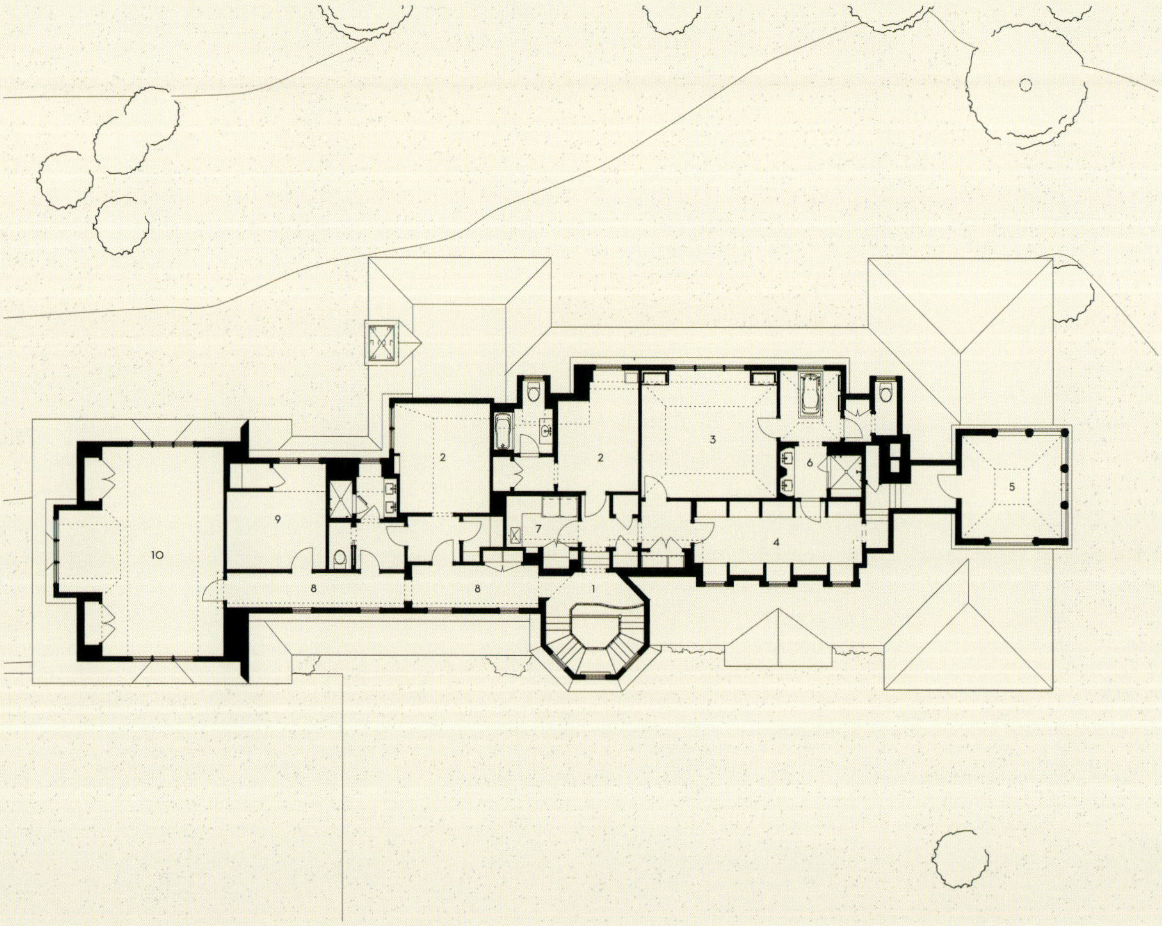

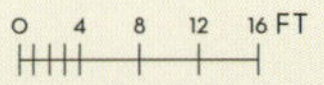

Spread 42-43, (Screened Porch), Bark walls, the random ashlar fireplace, and the bluestone floor all incorporate natural elements into the porch.

Page 45, (Deck), The screen porch opens onto a large deck, with views to the mountains.

–

Opposite, (Living Room), Natural woods, a river stone fireplace and details like peeled log beams all make the living room undeniably Adirondack.

This Page, (Kitchen), The kitchen opens to the dining room, which opens to the view.

–

(Deck), Even the balustrade and railing keep a roughhewn aspect, to make a deck in sympathy with the forest it frames.

–

(Mudroom), Storage, a brick floor, and fir beadboard walls make a mudroom. To maximize the view, the window sill is set low.

–

This Page, (Children's Rooms), Cozy bedrooms tuck into the eaves and dormers above.

Opposite, (Sleeping Porch), The parents tell us they spend all summer living on the screened-in sleeping porch.

Next Spread, (At Night), The stair tower on the front of the home emulates Adirondack fire towers.

–

Project Drawing, Olivia Rowan
Project Photography, Elizabeth Haynes

BUTTERFLY HOUSE

MUTTONTOWN
NEW YORK

The simple elegance of this home contrasts with the estates of its Long Island north shore neighbors. One of them, the sixty-room granite Hudson Estate, was once the home in exile of King Zog, Albania's last monarch. Another, the thirty-eight-room Chelsea Mansion – now a popular wedding venue – comes complete with towers and a moat. What interested our client was not the opulence of his former neighbors, but that the public now owns these estates, and has opened them as the five hundred and fifty acre Muttontown Preserve. Today these forests and meadows are full of nature paths, cross country ski routes, and horse trails. Perched on the edge of this protected heritage, at the beginning of those trails, our client wanted to build a stable for horses, and a home.

The site began as all scrub and brush, but it had good bones. A knoll for the home overlooks a flat meadow, ready for stables and exercise grounds for the horses.

Intrigued by the idea of building a home that did not follow a conventional shape and interested in capturing the best details of the Arts and Crafts Movement, our client suggested a butterfly plan, with four gable "wingtips" branching off from a central gable to make four arced sides to resemble, in plan, a butterfly. While the wings of the first known butterfly house, Westwood Park in Worcestershire, date to 1620, no houses followed until 1891, when Richard Norman Shaw enlarged 'The Chesters' with four wings at forty-five-degree angles. Calling it a 'double sun trap' for its maximal light and views, practitioners of the budding Arts and Crafts Movement quickly realized that here was a plan uniquely sympathetic to its context and nature. Edwin Lutyens tried a butterfly plan first at Papillon Hall in Leicestershire(1902). Named not for its plan but the client, a Huguenot family, Papillon was demolished in 1950. The best realization of a butterfly plan was at Edward Schroeder Prior's Voewood, in Norfolk (1905), a house still extant today.

In our home, the four arcs organize the site into four discrete exterior rooms, flowing off a central living room with views, a dominant hearth and lots of bookshelves. The private wing contains a study and bedrooms, with more bedrooms above. The other wing contains the kitchen, an octagonal dining room, a breakfast nook and a mudroom. Access to the garage is by a breezeway, part of a porch which wraps this half of the house, lending a permeability that engages the gardens and a wide double sweep of stone stairs leading to the stables down the hill.

Equal effort was made to create a comfortable home for the horses. Inspired by a Harrie T. Lindeberg-designed stable, the client liked the sleight of hand of a stable that does not reveal its full length on approach. We worked with a British firm specializing in equestrian stalls to make these accommodations functional, durable and elegant. Clerestory and eyebrow windows above echo the arched tops of the stall doors, while also providing light and ventilation. The low pitch of the roof and the modest ceiling above the stalls helps to reflect the radiant heat of the horses, avoiding a cold barn. The riding ring is centered on the stable with a viewing balcony above a lounge and kitchen.

Arts and Crafts grace notes abound; starting with the brick and wood shingle construction and sloping roofline and extending to the compressed windowpanes, the copper snow guards, and hardware like the olive knuckle hinges and brass door handles. As at Lutyens' Goddards, the verticals of the two chimneys are purposefully prominent and on axis. By contrast, the front door is intimately scaled and to one side, the glass rondels an inspiration from Baillie Scott. The effect of the house's five gables is of a tight knit village on a hill, presenting a different profile from every angle.

Reference: 'The Butterfly House' by Matthew Beckett, *Country Life*, Oct. 24, 2012.

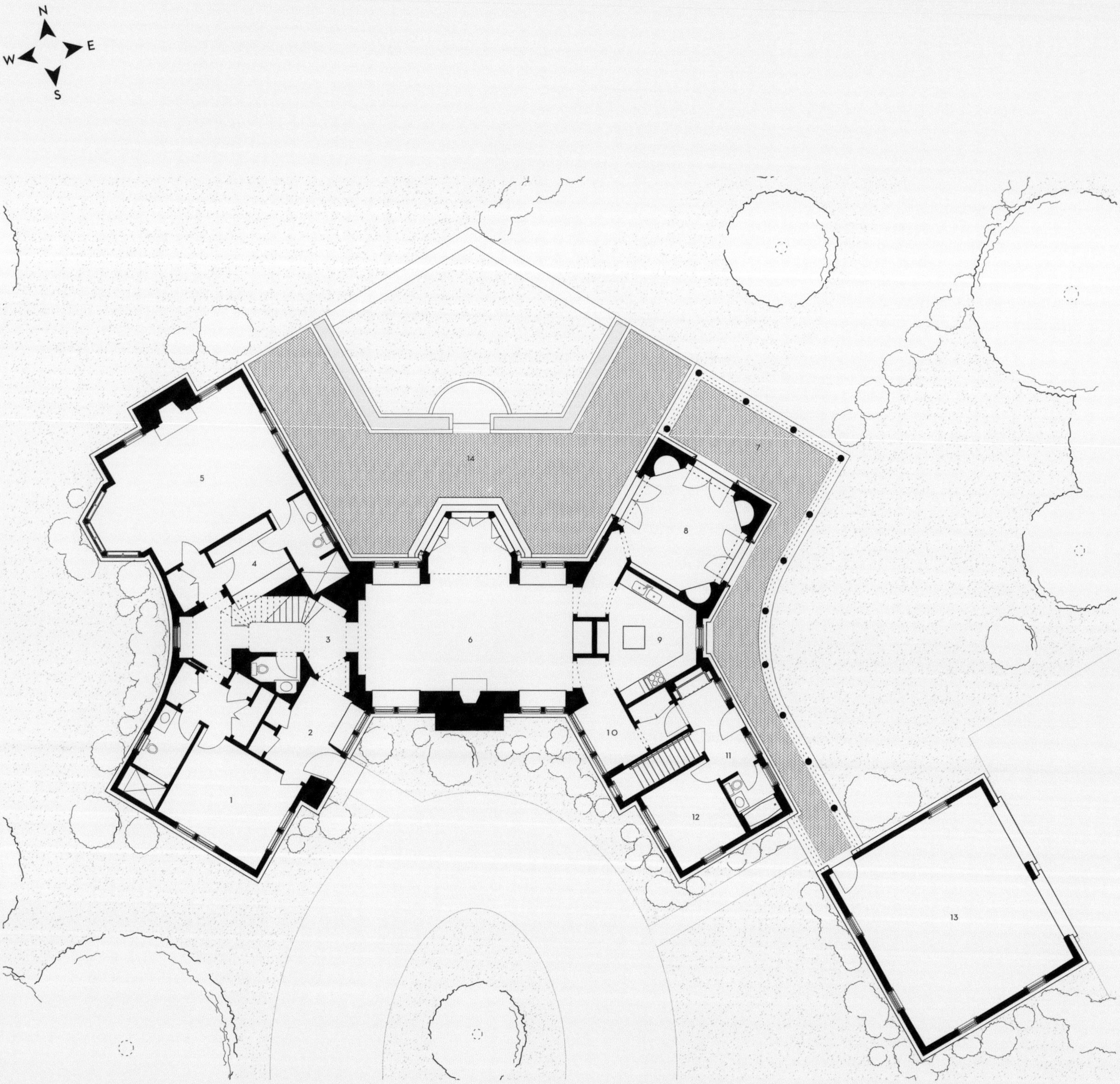

FIRST FLOOR

1. OFFICE
2. ENTRY FOYER
3. STAIR HALL
4. DRESSING ROOM
5. MASTER BEDROOM
6. LIVING ROOM
7. COVERED PORCH
8. DINING ROOM
9. KITCHEN
10. BREAKFAST NOOK
11. MUDROOM
12. MAID'S ROOM
13. GARAGE
14. PATIO

Spread 56-57, (Elevation), In a melding of English and American Arts and Crafts, the front door is moved off center.

Page 59, (Stair), The mahogany paneled stair hall resolves the geometry of the butterfly plan.

This Page, (Living Room), All parts of the home converge in its center, with a shallow vaulted ceiling.

SERAPHIM

–

Spread 62-63, (Exterior), The master bedroom is anchored by its chimney and bay window.

Opposite, (Stable Stall), Stalls imported from the United Kingdom imbue the barn with a grace as functionally durable as it is elegant.

This Page, (Stables), Clerestory and eyebrow windows above echo the rhythm of the horses' accommodations while also providing light and ventilation.

–

(Stable Exterior), The low pitch of the stable's roof and the modest ceiling above the stalls help to reflect the radiant heat of the horses, avoiding a cold barn.

–

(Horse Folly), This folly has a practical use: it encloses an equine treadmill.

–

Project Drawing,
John Mason
Project Photography,
Chuck Choi

COUNTRY ESTATE

OLD WESTBURY NEW YORK

This house began with its land – one hundred and twelve acres of it, near the north shore of Long Island. It had been on the block to be subdivided into as many as twenty-seven lots, and the community was happy when the client assumed stewardship of the whole piece. He had from a young age aspired to make his home there, and therefore it is not surprising that when he built, he started with the landscape designer, Ed Hollander, who then recommended our firm for the project. While establishing the fairways and greens for a private golf course, the plan for the property kept constant the overall volume of trees on the site, and preserved, maintained, and enhanced the existing equestrian easements. Working with Hollander and the client, we perched the house on the top of a gentle rise, orchestrating a winding approach road that would celebrate the house and the property.

The client's love of the landscape carries through to the home itself. We approached the house not as an object in a field, but rather as a frame, one that organizes its surroundings into a series of exterior rooms. They include an entry court, a discrete and more practical car court, a formal garden, a pool, and terraces that flow out onto the gardens, meadows and forest beyond. Arcades abutting these terraces blur hard lines between exterior and interior. A natural fall in the land posed not a problem but an opportunity: stairs come down it, leading to a high-ceilinged card room. As the house works its way around the pool, rooms become pergolas, and finally a whole pavilion with columns and pocketed louvered doors for walls, which creates a room in nature. Working with the site extended to the pragmatic aspects, too. For instance, a sophisticated geothermal heating and cooling system reduces energy consumption substantially.

Stylistically, the house is unabashedly Jacobean. The historically rigorous definition of Jacobean is that it was a transitional period in British house

architecture, between the Gothic exuberance of the Elizabethan prodigy house and the disciplined Renaissance Classicism of Inigo Jones. Put more simply, Jacobean condones both capitals and gargoyles. Its hybrid approach blends the columns and discipline of Classicism with the humanity and craft of Gothic. The language lends a home the range both to command the landscape around it and to create warm and intimate spaces within it.

For this home, major features are classically informed. The front door stands in the middle of the front facade, bringing the guest off a long allée and into an entry hall with a gracious central stair. Yet in its composition, the front of the house is purposefully asymmetrical - bays and gables were placed to achieve balance, not rigid symmetry. The house's material palette is warm but disciplined, comprising of hand-made brick with a sandy blush and carved Indiana limestone. Rigorous studies ensured that profiles and roofs come together fluently, without awkward junctions. At the same time, we had fun with some of the possibilities of Gothic. To resolve one corner, we used a turret. A bird house adorns a covered walkway's gable. And with the client's support and encouragement, we drew unique designs for the stone ornament and worked with a master stonemason from the National Cathedral to execute them.

Separated from the home by a stand of trees yet linked by a path going through the garden, a second house, a home for the client's mother, became a related project. We designed a place in sympathy with the first, but more intimate. Using an H plan, two wings flank a living room. While a profiled base of brick brings the house to the ground, the rest of the exterior walls are shingle. But from its French doors to its bay windows, to its deep eaves and columned porches, this home too still flows onto its terrace and the land.

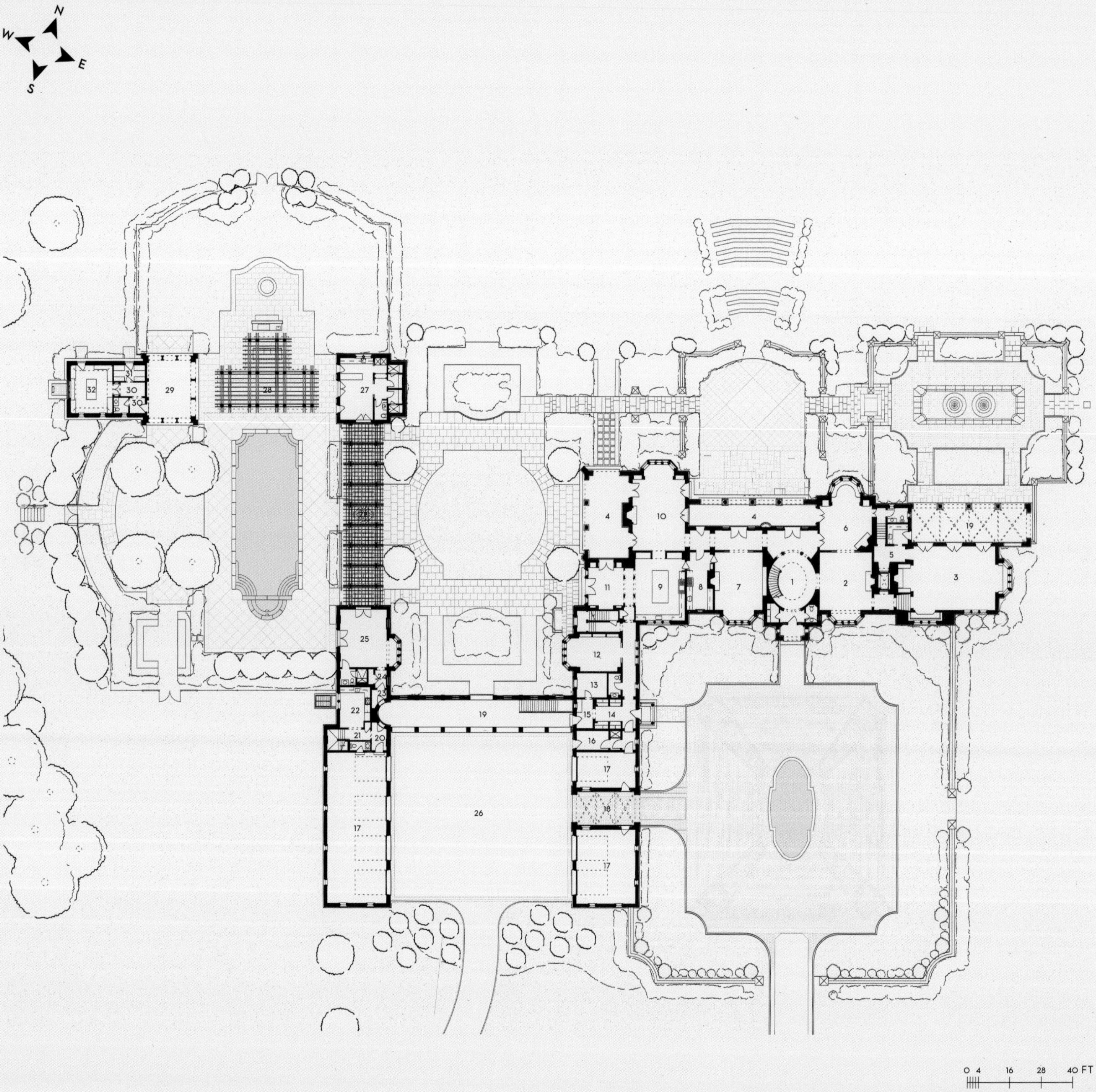

FIRST FLOOR

1. STAIR HALL
2. LIVING ROOM
3. CARD ROOM
4. PORCH
5. ELEVATOR HALL
6. DEN
7. DINING ROOM
8. PANTRY
9. KITCHEN
10. FAMILY ROOM
11. BREAKFAST ROOM
12. STUDY
13. OFFICE
14. MUDROOM
15. VESTIBULE
16. STORAGE
17. GARAGE
18. DRIVE THROUGH
19. LOGGIA
20. STAFF ENTRANCE
21. STAFF STAIR HALL
22. STAFF KITCHEN
23. GUEST ENTRY
24. GUEST HALL
25. GUEST BEDROOM
26. COURTYARD
27. POOL HOUSE
28. PERGOLA
29. POOL PAVILION
30. PRO-SHOP HALL
31. LOCKER ROOM
32. PRO-SHOP

–

Spread 70-71, (Northern Elevation), While composing the northern elevation, we aimed for balance while avoiding symmetry.

Page 73, (Loggia), As a style, Jacobean architecture blends the discipline of Classicism with the humanity and depth of Gothic.

–

Opposite (Stair Hall), We designed the laylight in the central stair hall with Thomas Finsterwald.

This Page (Living Room), A Gothic arch frames the living room, centered on its fireplace.

–

Top, (Kitchen), A light use of Gothic details, such as the leaded glass cabinets and columns below the island continues the spirit of the house.

Bottom, (Breakfast Room), The lattice work, canopy ceiling, and doors on two sides connect the breakfast room to the garden.

This Page, (Hallway), A wide hallway along the garden side connects the library to the family room.

–

Next Page, (Western Elevation), The landscape of the roof incorporates clay tiles, inset dormers, Jacobean chimney stacks, and the turret's patterned lead-coated copper.

N
W
E
S
MAINTENANCE
BUILDING
MAIN
ENTRANCE
GOLF
COURSE
POND
STONE BRIDGE
COTTAGE
POND
GUEST
HOUSE
TENNIS
PAVILION
SECONDARY
ENTRANCE
0 100 200 300 400 FT

1.

2.

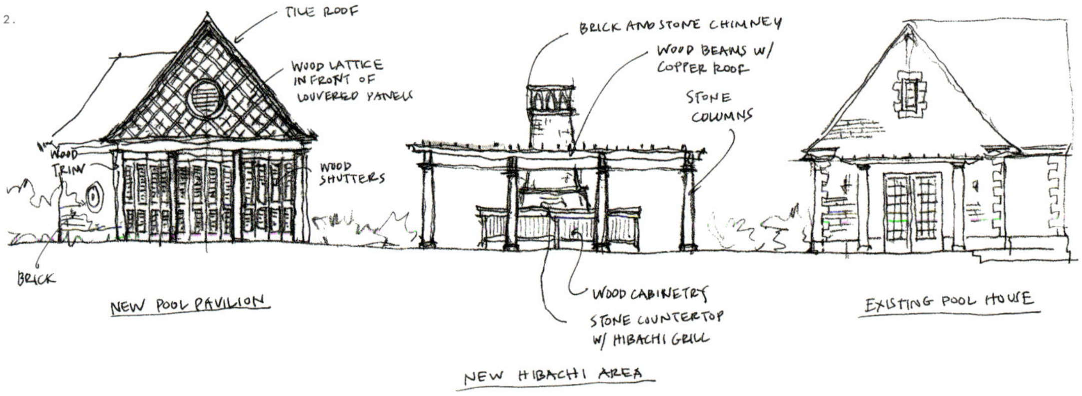
TILE ROOF
WOOD LATTICE IN FRONT OF LOUVERED PANELS
WOOD TRIM
WOOD SHUTTERS
BRICK
NEW POOL PAVILION
BRICK AND STONE CHIMNEY
WOOD BEAMS W/ COPPER ROOF
STONE COLUMNS
WOOD CABINETRY
STONE COUNTERTOP W/ HIBACHI GRILL
NEW HIBACHI AREA
EXISTING POOL HOUSE

3.

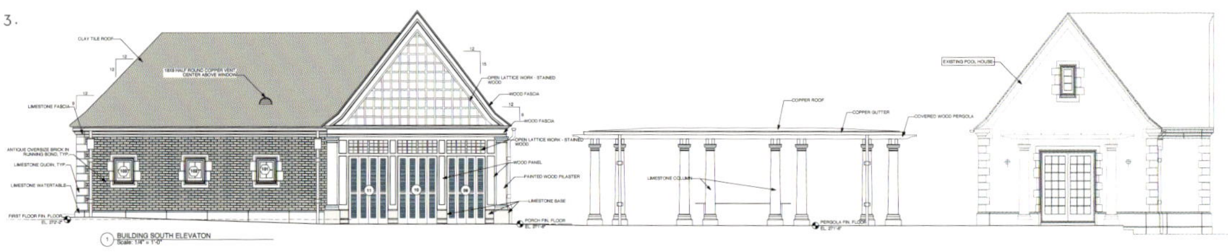

4.

5.

6.

1. CONCEPT SKETCH
2. RESOLVED SKETCH
3. WORKING DRAWINGS
4. ARBOR PERSPECTIVE
5. ARBOR, AS BUILT
6. LATTICE PAVILION

PROCESS. POOL PAVILIONS

The iterative process of designing the pool and its supporting pavilions started by treating it as another room, which happened to be outside. Working it into the logic of the house meant a respect for symmetry and axes. The disciplined and gradual resolution of the design through two-dimensional elevations and perspective sketches yielded a sequence of inter-connected spaces.

–

Opposite, This Page & Next Spread (Pool),
The pool and its pavilions, on a summer evening.

–

Project drawing, John Mason
Project photography, Chuck Choi

REIMAGINING DELANO & ALDRICH

OLD WESTBURY
NEW YORK

How do you understate grandeur? Though this house was built on an estate that once covered nearly two hundred acres, there is no vast lawn or unobstructed approach – it is tucked into the woods, to emerge only around the last bend of its driveway. At first glance, the brick elevation appears simple, but the bottom line of windows is a full two stories tall. That height was used by the original architects, Delano & Aldrich, to create a set of state rooms of straightforward elegance; full advantage was taken of the high ceilings, but they are not flaunted. A masterful plan ties it all together. A transom window above the front door bathes the entry hall in light, a door slips below the vertiginous main stair, and an ingenious circular vestibule negotiates between the library and living room.

However, it was a house of its time, of 1930. There was a whole wing for servants, and the other wing was a ground floor suite. Our clients have a big and active family, and while they cherished the comfortable formality of the state rooms, they needed more informal spaces to congregate.

Working with the decorator Steven Gambrel, we brought the house up to date. The entire bedroom wing became a family room. Extra height was found in the ceiling above it, allowing a new ribbed barrel vault, after the legendary yellow drawing room John Fowler designed with Nancy Lancaster for her home on Avery Row in London. By turning a hallway and bath into a tucked-in bar, a path was found to directly link the new room to the rest of the home.

Some of the most dramatic work happened in the service wing. Here the focal point became the kitchen, which moved from the front to the back of the house. It was our client's inspiration to take out two small servant rooms on the second floor, so the kitchen could soar into the space above. A new door gives the kitchen direct access to the breakfast room

and the dining room beyond. A simple circular vestibule, echoing one from Delano & Aldrich, ties the kitchen back to the house's main axis. These curves on the ground floor are repeated above, where a second circular vestibule ties together the children's rooms, and an oval centers the master bath. Toward the garden, the new kitchen opens onto the work of another renovation, a greenhouse that harkens to the 1970s. Rather than demolishing it to build a new conservatory, the clients decided to honor this part of the house's history. With some attention to details and finishes, it became half plant-room, half family-room, and is today one of the family's favorite spaces.

Beyond and behind these major alterations were countless acts of fine tuning. For the bar, an existing skylight was redirected through the space between roof and ceiling to spill its rays into the middle of the room. The breakfast room received new plasterwork and pilasters. A new doorway between the dining room and living room allows the breakfast room, dining room, and living room to be traversed *en filade*. A new 'secret door,' carrying a complete bookshelf on its hinges, provides quick access from the family room into the library. Central air came to the whole house for the first time, which was enormously difficult as the floors are concrete with terracotta infill. Air conditioning and speakers were invisibly inserted into the living room. New ducts reached out underground to condition the greenhouse, making it livable in the dead of winter. Across the grounds nothing was added, and everything was renovated, including the pool, tennis court, pool house, and garage – where an apartment is on the renovated second floor.

We are often called upon to draft a good plan from scratch, or to fix a bad plan, but it may be our greatest pleasure – and the most difficult work – to improve upon a plan that is already quite good.

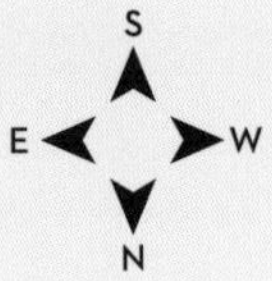

EXISTING FIRST FLOOR

1. MAIN STAIR HALL
2. BACK STAIR HALL
3. ENTRY
4. HALL
5. BEDROOM
6. SCREENED PORCH
7. LIBRARY
8. LIVING ROOM
9. DINING ROOM
10. BREAKFAST ROOM
11. CONSERVATORY
12. GREENHOUSE
13. STAFF LOUNGE
14. STAFF STAIR HALL
15. BUTLER'S PANTRY
16. CLOAK ROOM
17. KITCHEN
18. STAFF PORCH

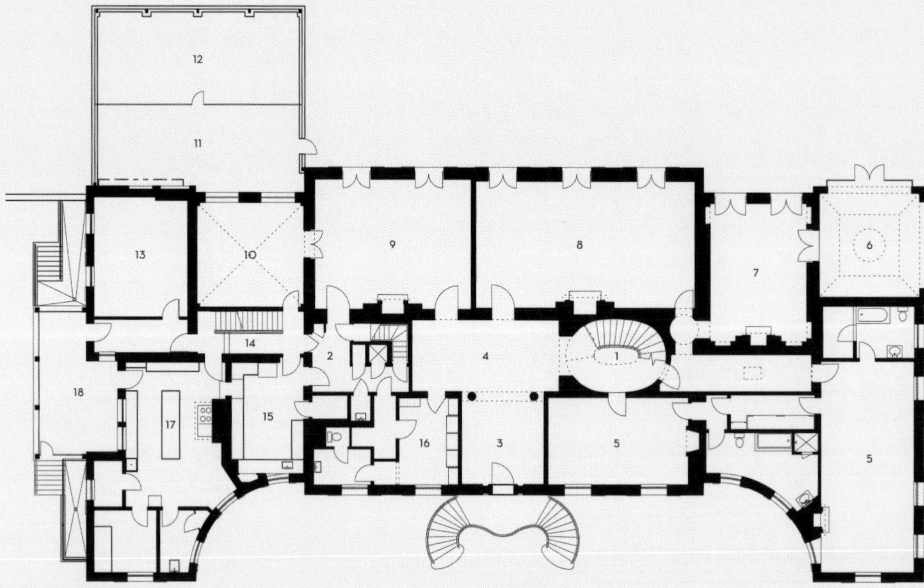

COMPLETED FIRST FLOOR

1. MAIN STAIR HALL
2. BACK STAIR HALL
3. ENTRY
4. HALL
5. OFFICE
6. BAR
7. FAMILY ROOM
8. SCREENED PORCH
9. LIBRARY
10. LIVING ROOM
11. DINING ROOM
12. BREAKFAST ROOM
13. KITCHEN
14. BUTLER'S PANTRY
15. PANTRY
16. CLOAK ROOM
17. MUD ROOM
18. STAFF OFFICE
19. STAFF PORCH
20. CONSERVATORY
21. GREEN HOUSE

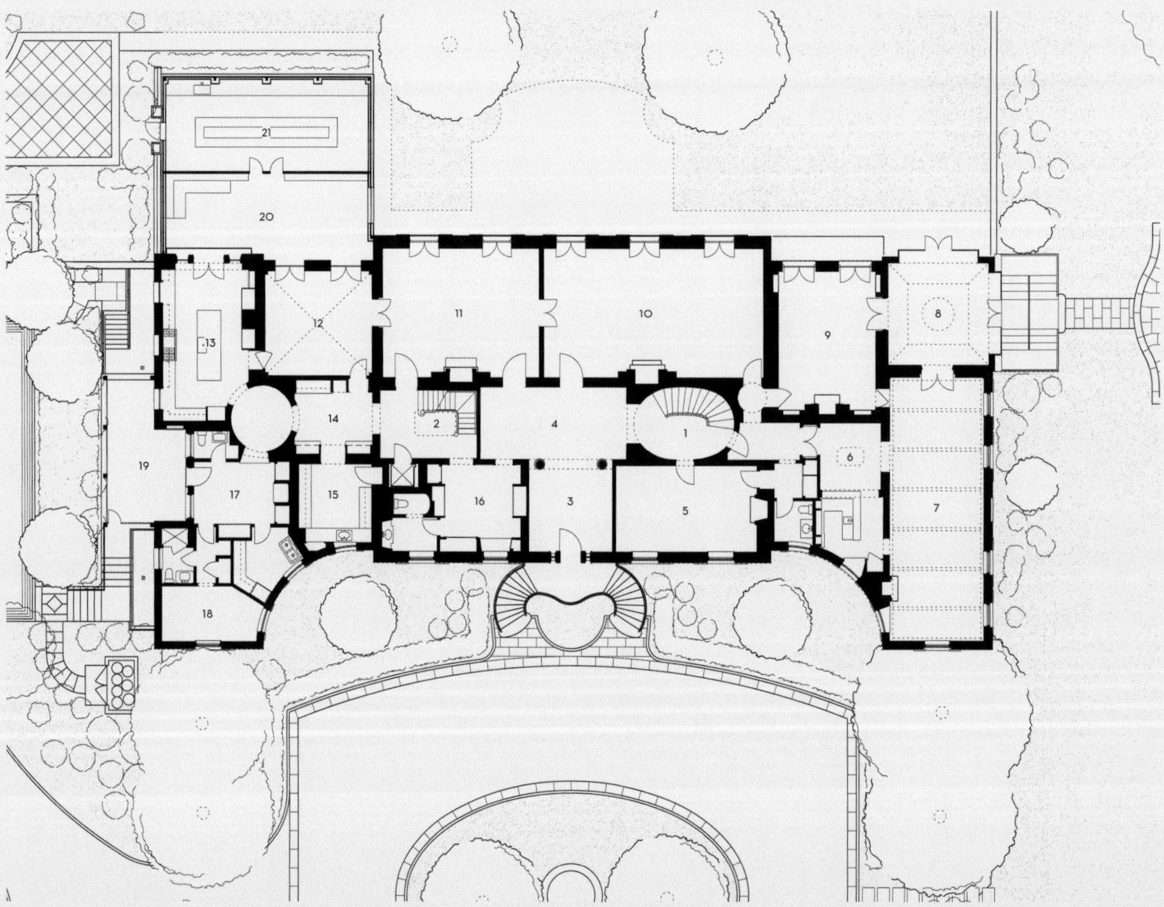

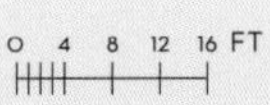

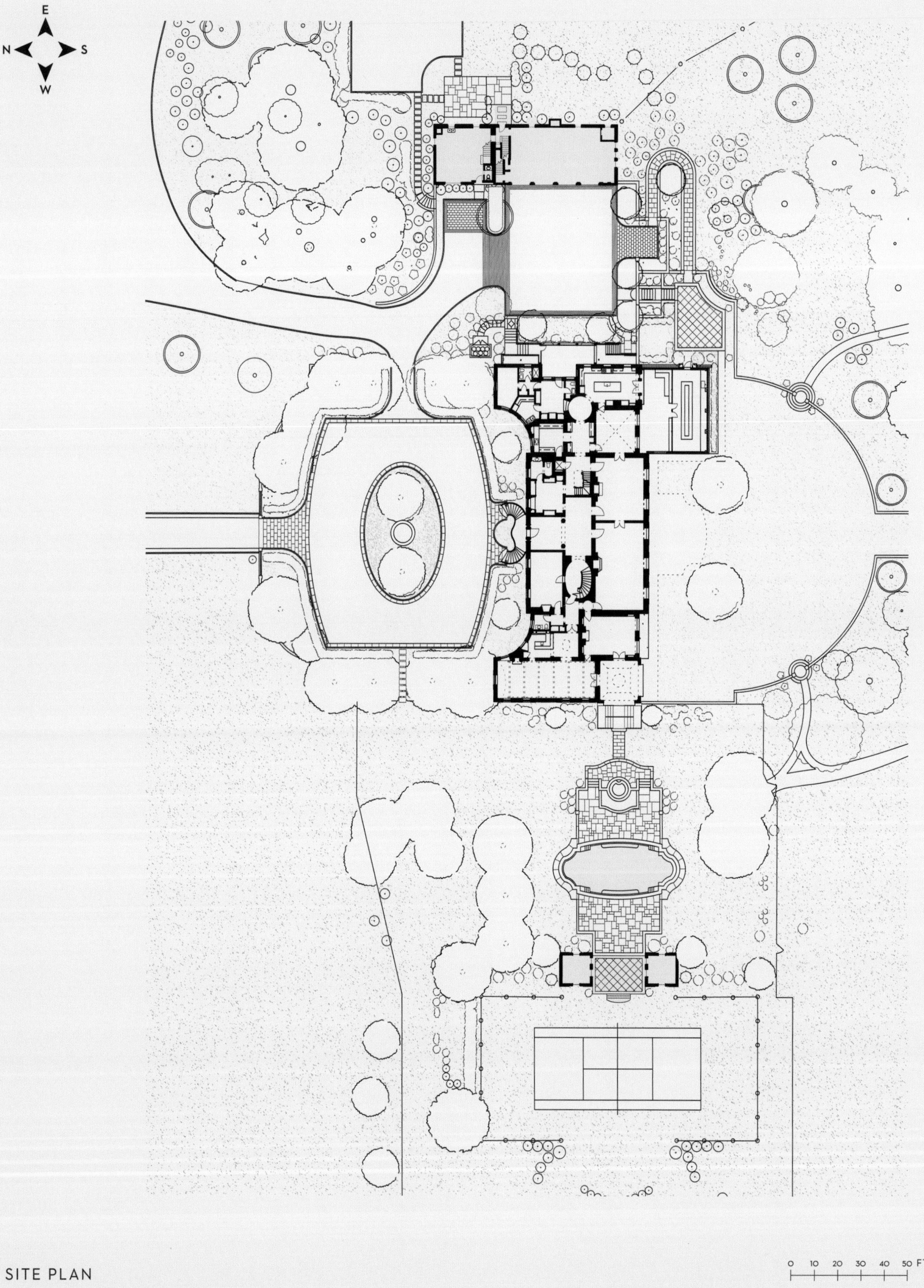

SITE PLAN

–

Page 87, (Stair), The family room is accessed through a portal tucked below the Delano & Aldrich stair.

Page 89, (Office), A former bedroom became a family office with a russet red ceiling.

–

Opposite, (Dining), The dining room of the original house was restored, connecting it to the living room so the grand rooms now connect *en filade*.

This Page, (Living), Completely restoring the living room enabled mechanical and audio systems to be inserted.

–

Opposite, (Kitchen), It was our client's inspiration to take out two small servant rooms on the second floor, so the kitchen could soar into the space above.

This Page Left, (Kitchen), The new curved wall in the corner of the kitchen is common with the circular vestibule that connects kitchen, back entry, mudroom and pantry.

This Page Right, (Original Vestibule), This circular vestibule connects the living room, library and stair hall to the family room.

–

(Cloak Room), The ceiling of this room had been dropped below its window head –its full height was reclaimed and now its red lacquered walls, black accents, and sconces provide guests ample space to hang their coats and adjust their attire.

–

(Mudroom), A practical room in muted tones adjacent to the back door is ready for the boots, coats, and mud for the home's less formal entrances.

–

(Library), The library reconfigured as a game room connects by hidden doors to the living room and family room.

–

(Family Room), A first-floor suite was converted into a more casual gathering place for the family. Extra height found in the ceiling above allowed a new ribbed barrel vault.

2.

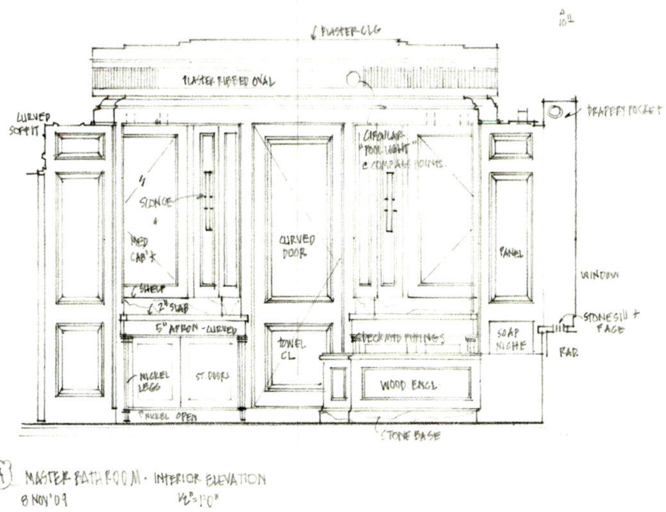

3.

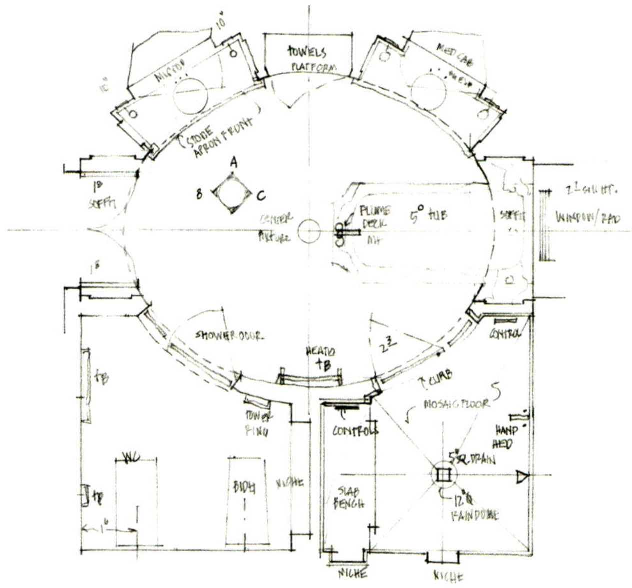

4.

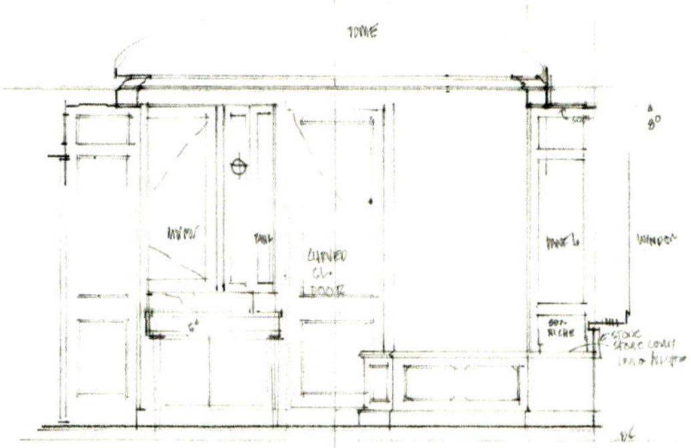

5.

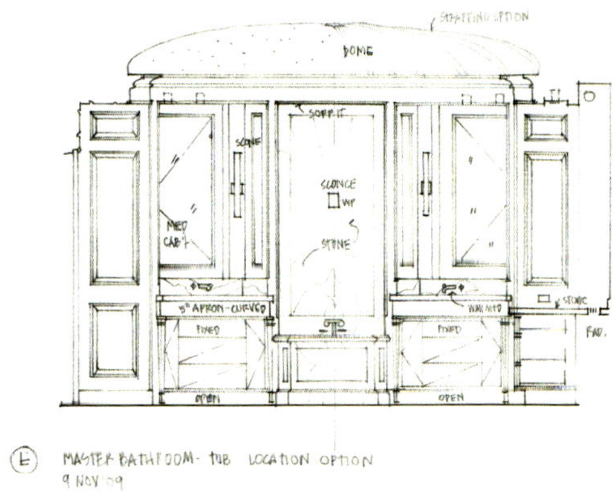

6.

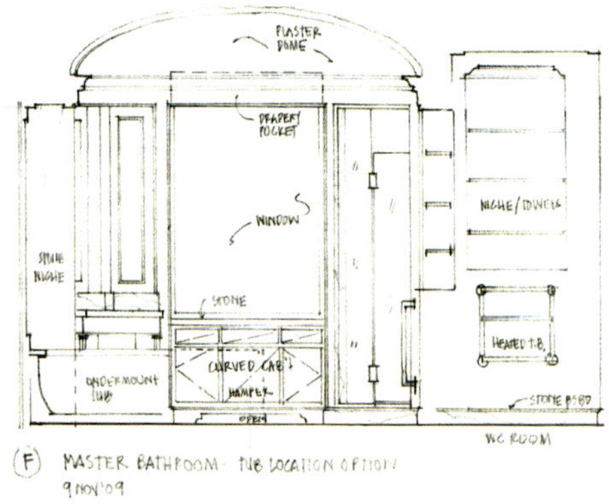

7.

PROCESS.

Every architect has to pick their battles, even Delano & Aldrich. While the downstairs formal rooms were spectacular, everything else was simpler – to the point of a wine rack in the basement made from scrap boards with penciled notes and V-cuts for the bottles. The renovation was an opportunity to bring some of the style of those first-floor rooms into the rest of the house. Upstairs, we worked through a series of plans, elevations and perspective sketches to develop a master bath with a quarter matched Italian marble floor around which the full master suite could center.

1. THE BATHROOM, AS BUILT
2. ELEVATION SKETCH
3. PLAN ITERATION
4. ELEVATION SKETCH
5. ELEVATION SKETCH
6. ELEVATION SKETCH
7. PERSPECTIVE SKETCH

–

Project drawing, John Mason
Project photography, Eric Piasecki

CITY

EAST RIVER DUPLEX

GRACIE SQUARE
MANHATTAN

It is often hard to tell, among its canyons and caves, that Manhattan is an island. Not so here. This apartment came with a sweeping view up and down the East River, dramatically framed by a corner of glass in its living room. The apartment also came with a lot of idiosyncrasies.

The dawn of the grand apartment building in New York was a period of great experimentation, a time that left us with buildings imbued with eccentricities and whimsy rarely seen in today's more standard constructions. This building has two different entrances, a marbled and columned crown, and started life with a dock for yachts at the base. For good measure, there is also a block-spanning covered drive for cars. The idiosyncrasy that most affected this apartment was that the building has different wings, both the same total height, but with different numbers of floors. In our apartment, the portion with commanding views of the river, holding the living and dining rooms, has appropriately high ceilings. Coming off its back are wings for bedrooms with more floors than the main wing, lower ceiling heights than the main wing, and therefore floors that mis-align with the main wing. To navigate the misalignment, our apartment came with two short flights of steps from the formal rooms in the front to the two floors of bedrooms, in the building's back.

The apartment itself can be understood as three parts. First, there are the formal rooms – living, dining, and library – in the main wing, facing the river. For them, we focused on creating a sequence of distinct spaces. The dining room became an octagon – in its high ceiling nestles a Soane-inspired oculus. Strategically placed columns lend the living room a sense of balance and symmetry that makes that most spectacular moment – the glass corner – a surprise. The library connects directly to the living room through a door that is subtle but natural. Rich colors, one of the many contributions

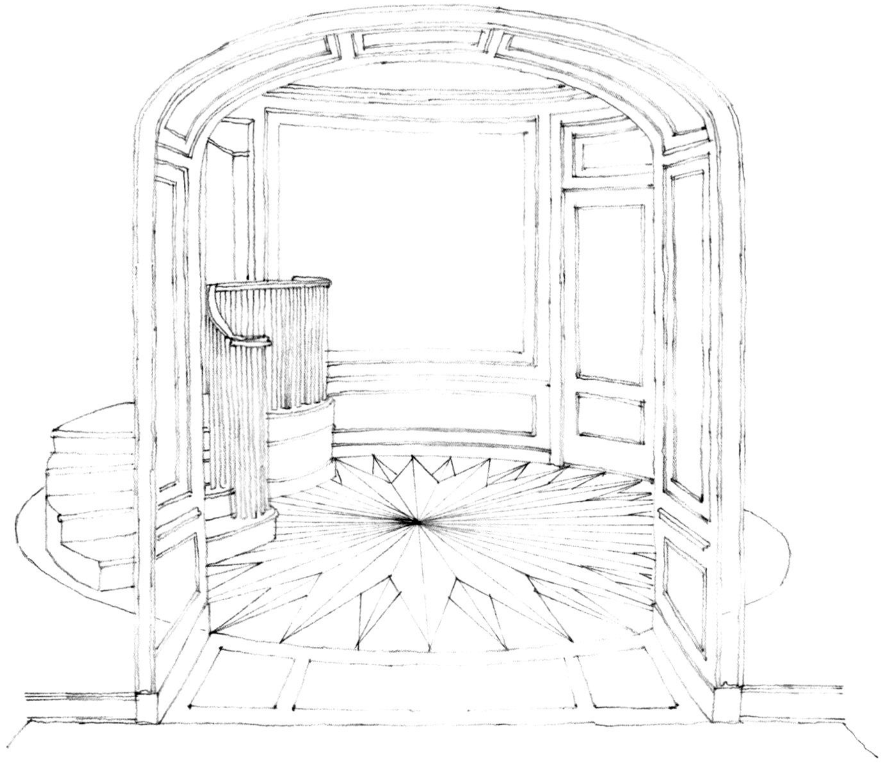

of designer Tony Ingrao, provide a welcome sense of repose in contrast to the ever-changing river beyond. Thickened walls allowed both built-in cabinetry and bookcases as well as space to hide the essential ducts and other services essential to keeping a modern home fully functional, without interrupting the rooms they service.

Second, there is the service area – on the same level and also in the main wing but facing the building's courtyard. Here, we made the kitchen a more social place, ripping out a hallway of storage to create a true family room, a rarity in an old New York apartment. A breakfast nook enjoys the morning light.

Finally, the two floors of bedrooms are up the stairs in the back of the building. Relationships between them were fine-tuned. A set of dressing rooms were designed to adjoin the master bedroom. Bathrooms were modernized and properly paired. A passage between the study and the master bedroom flipped a bathroom, to give it a window and a view out.

All three parts come together in the oval entrance off of the private elevator vestibule. It is the fulcrum around which the entire apartment turns. By making it an oval, the room could absorb and combine entrances to the three different parts of the home. We took pleasure and inspiration from the challenges of detailing the space. Each door was specially made to curve with its surface. The wall paneling and moldings were formed from a hard plaster. The interstitial spaces created by inserting the oval into a rectangular plan provided room for a bar and wine storage, crafted from Cerejeira, adjacent to the library. The clients wanted to enjoy even emphasize – the level change between the bedroom wings in the back and the rest of the apartment. We worked with them to add a small balcony to the stairs, with a well-detailed railing. A small staircase and balcony celebrate – even have fun with – the level change between the bedroom wing and the rest of the apartment.

EXISTING LOWER FLOOR

1. PLAY ROOM
2. HALL
3. BEDROOM
4. GYM
5. STAFF BEDROOM

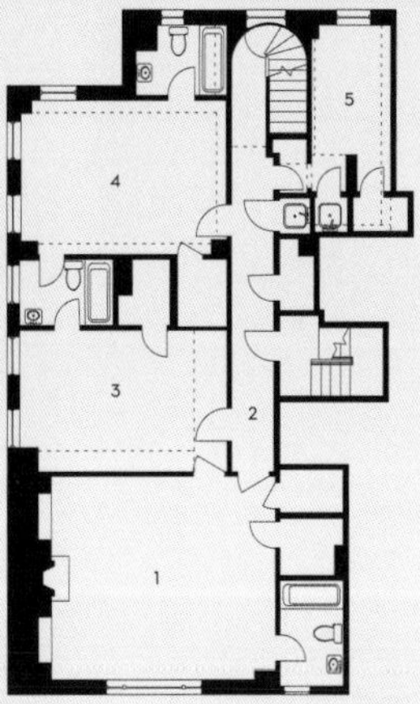

EXISTING UPPER FLOOR

1. FAMILY ROOM
2. LIVING ROOM
3. DINING ROOM
4. KITCHEN
5. BREAKFAST ROOM
6. PANTRY
7. MECHANICAL CLOSET
8. HALL
9. MASTER BEDROOM
10. HER DRESSING ROOM
11. HIS DRESSING ROOM
12. MASTER BATHROOM
13. LIBRARY
14. BALCONY
15. ENTRY GALLERY

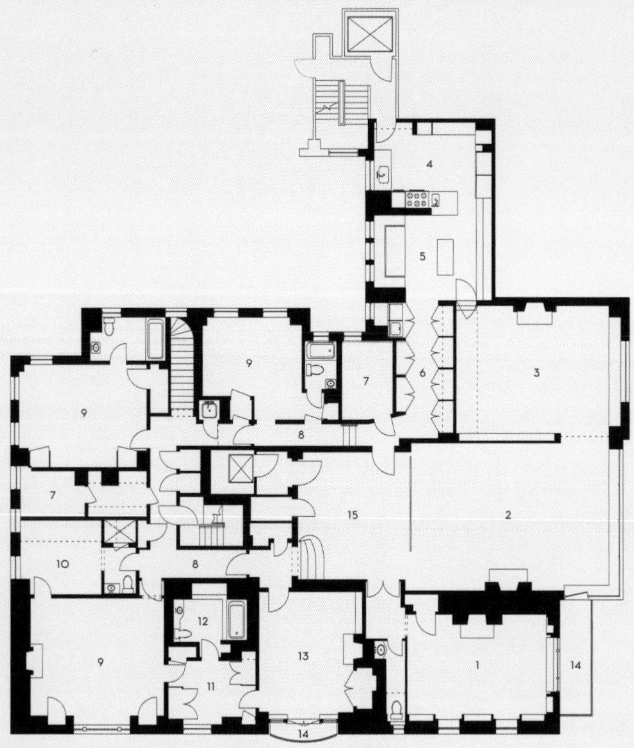

COMPLETED LOWER FLOOR

1. PLAY ROOM
2. HALL
3. BEDROOM
4. OFFICE

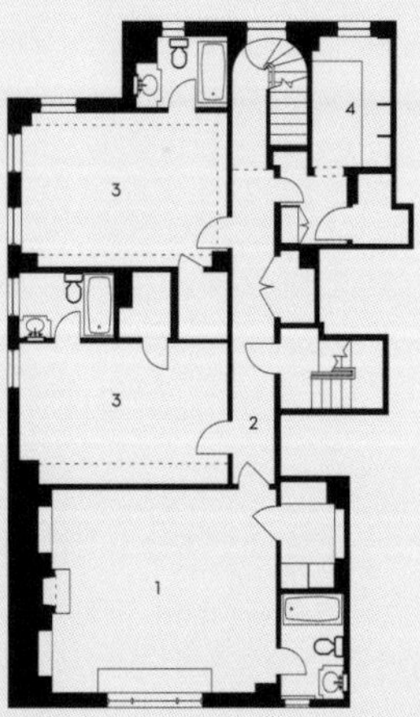

COMPLETED UPPER FLOOR

1. LIBRARY
2. LIVING ROOM
3. DINING ROOM
4. PANTRY/LAUNDRY ROOM
5. KITCHEN
6. FAMILY ROOM
7. HALL
8. MAID'S BEDROOM
9. MECHANICAL CLOSET
10. GUEST BEDROOM
11. MASTER BEDROOM
12. HER DRESSING ROOM
13. HER MASTER BATHROOM
14. HIS DRESSING ROOM
15. HIS MASTER BATHROOM
16. HIS STUDY
17. BALCONY
18. GALLERY
19. ELEVATOR VESTIBULE
20. BAR

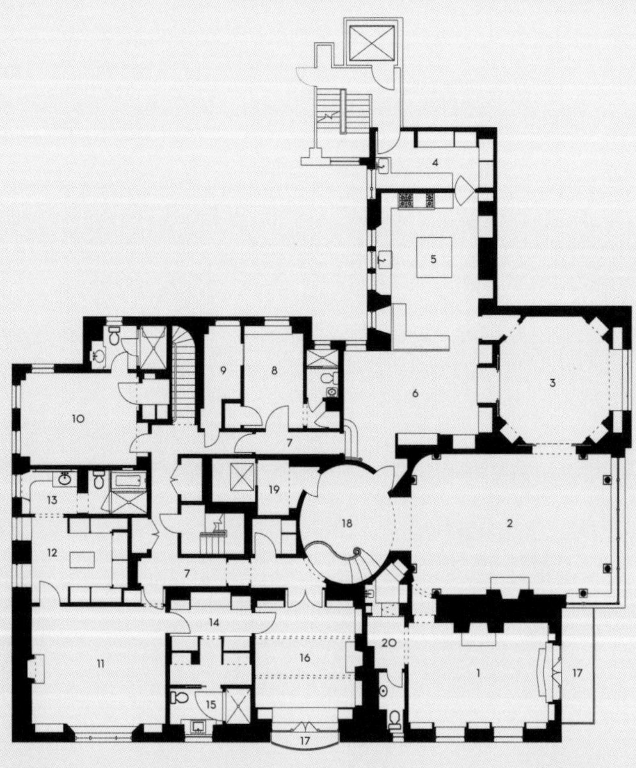

0 4 8 12 16 FT

Spread 104-105, (Library), From the corners of this apartment, it is possible to look both up and down the East River.

Page 107, (Bar), The interstitial spaces created by inserting the oval into a rectangular plan provided room for a bar and wine storage.

This Page, (Kitchen), Removing a hallway of closets created a generous kitchen and family room, a rarity for New York.

This Page, (Study), The study offers a retreat, mediating the transition from the private realm of the bedrooms.

Opposite, (Dining Room), The octagonal dining room space between two large structural beams was recaptured to make a Soane-inspired lantern ceiling.

–

(Living Room), We curved the corners of the living room, to allow for the subtle insertion of a passage to the library.

–

Project drawing, Rita Marks
Project photography, Scott Morris of SGM
Additional photography, Nicolas Kemper

1.

2.

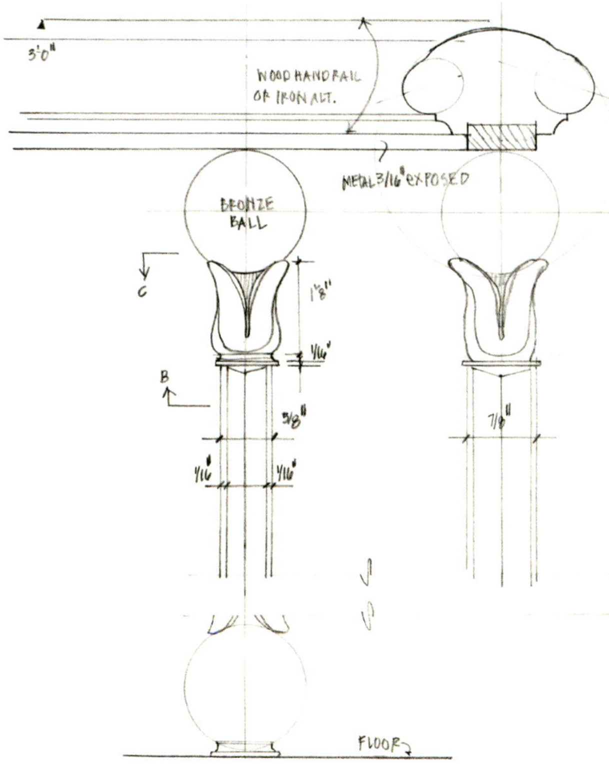

PROCESS.

Inspired by the detail from a broken umbrella, a bronze drapery rod, and collaborations with a talented blacksmith, the eventual resolution of the front stair's railing came after a series of detailed sketches.

1. RAILING FEET, AS BUILT
2. RAILING SKETCH ELEVATION
3. ROOM PERSPECTIVE SKETCH
4. RAILING TIE, AS BUILT

3.

4.

CENTRAL PARK DUPLEX

UPPER WEST SIDE
NEW YORK

How do you keep it simple?

In command of tree top views across Central Park, this apartment came with pre-war charm, such as high ceilings and generous windows. The apartment also came with pre-war shortcomings, such as no-air conditioning, small bathrooms, and a duplex arrangement that left the formal rooms down a staircase from the rest of the apartment. Not only did the apartment begin split across two floors, it also began literally split. The client had bought a neighboring, unattached apartment.

Our family was clear they wanted a clean and contemporary home. We have, in some of our projects, worked with craftspeople to include carved stone, intricate floors, sculptural geometries, and columns of every order, but here our clients wanted to keep it simple and serene. Working with the family and the decorator Eve Robinson, a visually peaceful palette was pulled together. Light woods, white walls and blue accents composed together an interior simple but not plain. Joints were minimized. In the kitchen, a talented millworker and equally talented stone fabricator worked with us to seamlessly integrate disparate materials with flush joints and a carefully managed hierarchy of transitions in material and function.

It would, however, be a mistake to think simplicity the opposite of complexity, or to equate simple with easy. Life is endlessly complex, the life of a home especially so. Realizing simplicity in a home, therefore, requires thoughtful and nuanced effort.

Simplicity starts with the plan. The apartment's two floors allowed it to be organized like a house. The kitchen and formal rooms are on the first floor, private bedrooms, a study, and a family room are above. Starting with such a clear natural partition allowed for the consequent removal of most artificial partitions. When removing walls, we applied the hide-and-seek rule. Any child instinctually knows that a good game of hide-and-seek requires rooms with two exits – a door for the person 'it' to enter, and a door for everyone else to flee. Even if the

participants are more tactful with their entrances and exits, a successful party, or even family gathering, has similar spatial requirements. Therefore, the apartment's beginning, its foyer, connects without interruption to the stair, the living room, the dining room, the kitchen, and back to the foyer. On the second story, what had been the partitioning line between the two different apartments became the heart of the private quarters. A double closet between the apartments gave way to create a book lined vestibule at the back door. Two symmetrical pocket doors inserted into the wall of the family room allowed entrance by both the vestibule and *en filade*, from the study. The generous plan allows for a second-floor family living room, a private study, a small gym, and plenty of bedrooms.

A better plan does not always mean fewer walls. By example, the addition of a wall at the front door takes the guest straight into the foyer, and the rest of the apartment beyond.

A better plan does not mean haphazard rooms. Choices of materials and details as subtle as the location of a portal, bookshelf, counter or closet all, properly coordinated, lend each room distinct definition and character. Those distinctions allow rooms to serve gatherings large and small and the growth and congregation of families.

Having established the plan, simplicity rests on the details. Walls became thicker to define spaces and doorways but do double duty, providing space for new air conditioning ducts, storage, built in shelves and cabinets. Doors tuck into pockets and portals. Lines rigorously carry through and between those shelves and cabinets. Everywhere a wall meets the ceiling, simple taut moldings reference tradition but are not slaves to it. Sometimes they conceal air conditioning grills.

In sum, simplicity is making the things we have to do serve the thing we want to do. Like when the stair railing glides to the floor like a curling piece of paper.

–

(Stair), The stair railing curls to the floor like the curled piece of paper that was its inspiration.

—

(Foyer to Dining), A glass door and partition separate the living and dining rooms while still allowing light to flood through the apartment.

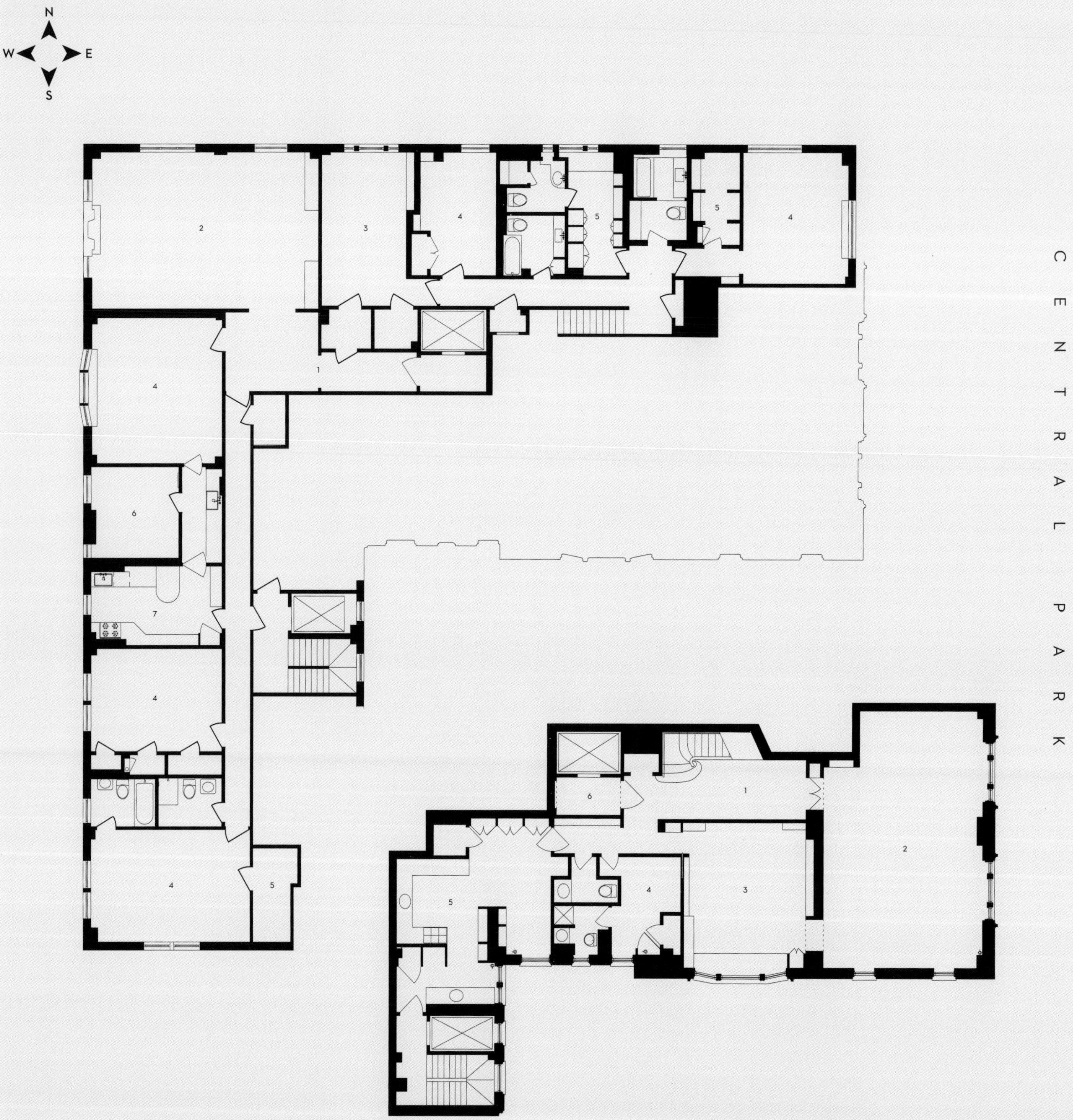

EXISTING 9TH FLOOR

1. ENTRY HALL
2. LIVING ROOM
3. STUDY
4. BEDROOM
5. CLOSET
6. STORAGE
7. LAUNDRY

EXISTING 8TH FLOOR

0 4 8 12 16 FT

1. ENTRY HALL
2. LIVING ROOM
3. DINING ROOM
4. MAID'S ROOM
5. KITCHEN
6. ELEVATOR VESTIBULE

COMPLETED 9TH FLOOR

1. FAMILY ROOM
2. STUDY
3. HER DRESSING ROOM
4. MASTER BATHROOM
5. HIS DRESSING ROOM
6. MASTER BEDROOM
7. VESTIBULE
8. BEDROOM
9. MECHANICAL ROOM
10. LAUNDRY

COMPLETED 8TH FLOOR

1. STAIR HALL
2. LIVING ROOM
3. DINING ROOM
4. KITCHEN
5. BUTLER'S PANTRY
6. ELEVATOR VESTIBULE

–

(Dining Room), The banquette and expanding table allow flexible seating for gatherings small and large.

Walker Evans
CUBISM

–

(Dining to Foyer), The glass partition, designed by Eve Robinson, displays art, provides storage, and hides a television.

–

(Kitchen), A talented millworker and equally talented stone fabricator worked with us to seamlessly integrate disparate materials with flush joints.

–

(Study), On the second floor, blue lacquered shelves display books, while elm cabinets conceal everything else.

Left, (Study), The cabinetwork provides a niche for the couch, and space for a vent above.

Right, (Dressing Room), The dressing room provides a calm well-ordered home for each item of clothing, and a spectacular mirror, centered in front of the window.

Next Spread, (Living Room), The furniture draws its colors from the blue sky and the caramel and green of Central Park.

Project drawing, Rita Marks
Project photography, Eric Piasecki

CALATRAVA

WEST END AVENUE AERIE

UPPER WEST SIDE
NEW YORK

Flow is a word often thrown around in describing homes, used so often that it sometimes lacks content – presumably it is a good thing, but what does it actually mean? Simply fewer walls? How does a space flow?

In nature, flow happens between opposites. Hot air flows to cool regions, water flows from above to below, electrons flow between opposite charges. Flow happens between places in tension, places that are different. In short, just because a space has no barriers does not mean we want to cross to the other side.

This home began with an apartment in a new building with glorious sweeping views across the Hudson River. As the apartment's first resident, however, our client inherited a developer plan. One entered into a substantial but windowless foyer. The dining room was near the entrance to the apartment and three rooms away from the kitchen. All of the rooms were approximately the same. Though they had ample doors and hallways between them, there was no flow. The rooms needed a hierarchy, needed differentiation, so, like water cascading from pool to pool, there would be a natural movement across and through them.

We orchestrated, with interior designer Bunny Williams, a complete renovation. The entrance foyer was reimagined and reorganized to capture windows, light and view. Space was created for a piano. Generous walls spread out for art. The high gloss ceiling creates the illusion of infinite height in a space with infinite views. A large wide doorway was created to give access to the expanded living room. Here the details are firm but spare. There are ample opportunities to sit. While anchored by a fireplace, the room's focus will always be the corner views out across the West Side and onto the Hudson River beyond. A bright palette – white walls and even a chrome mantle – leave the focus on the view. Expanding that view by borrowing from the adjacent room, a double door connects

to that space, the dining room. Contrasting with the living room, the dining room is warm, with shelves, books, and a seating cluster. From there, a single door connects to the kitchen, where bright surfaces are in sympathy with its corner position and its function. The kitchen was also reorganized and reimagined. All of its equipment came off of the exterior wall to create a clear path. By contrast, linking the kitchen back to the front hall is a compact but elegant bar clad in a richly hued wood.

A careful division between public and personal was made at the new entry foyer where a curved and pocketing door leads into the private realm. These rooms have a destination. Off the master bedroom, in command of the building's curved corner window, is the owner's study, engaged with the city beyond.

As with all projects, much of the resolution happened in the parts unseen. Many walls and doors moved. Many of the walls even became thicker. With their extra thickness, they could accommodate ducts and mechanical equipment that had previously all been in the ceiling. What remained could then be rerouted over secondary spaces to maximize ceiling height in the main spaces.

The door into the front hall is perfectly aligned on the centerline between two windows, and even subtly curved. No one sells fire rated curved doors, so we commissioned a custom calcified plaster door. It took two or three tries before they got it right. But to achieve something so perfect, we had also to do something downright quirky. The elevator corridor was not built perfectly on axis with the entry door. To correct the misalignment, the entrance jogs a foot within its deep jamb.

After all, the tension between spaces cool and warm, spacious and cozy, perfect and a bit quirky, are what brings the apartment to life, and sets it in motion.

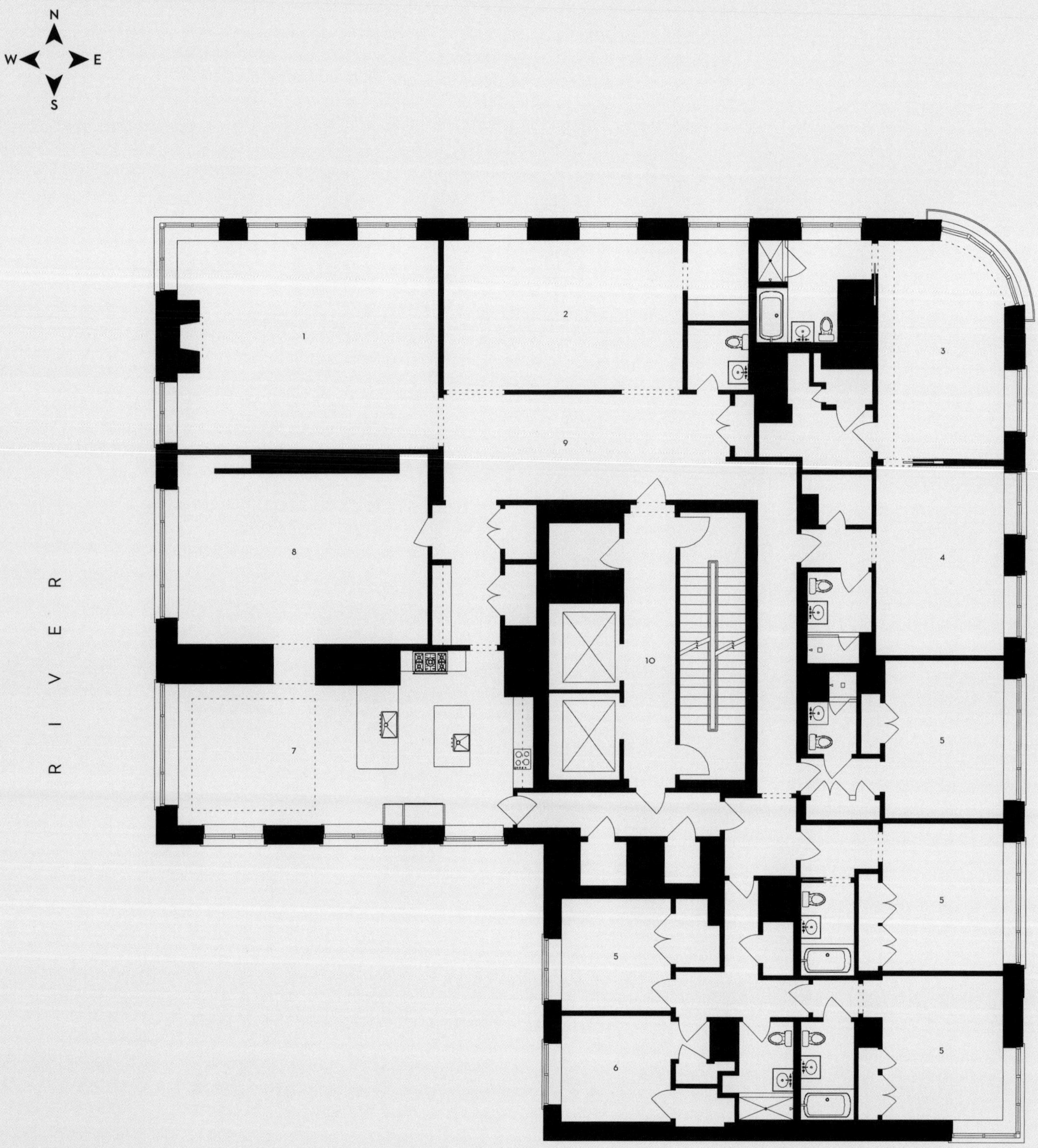

EXISTING FLOOR PLAN

0 4 8 12 16 FT

1. LIVING ROOM
2. DINING ROOM
3. MASTER BEDROOM
4. SITTING ROOM
5. BEDROOM
6. SITTING ROOM
7. KITCHEN
8. FAMILY ROOM
9. FOYER
10. ENTRY HALL

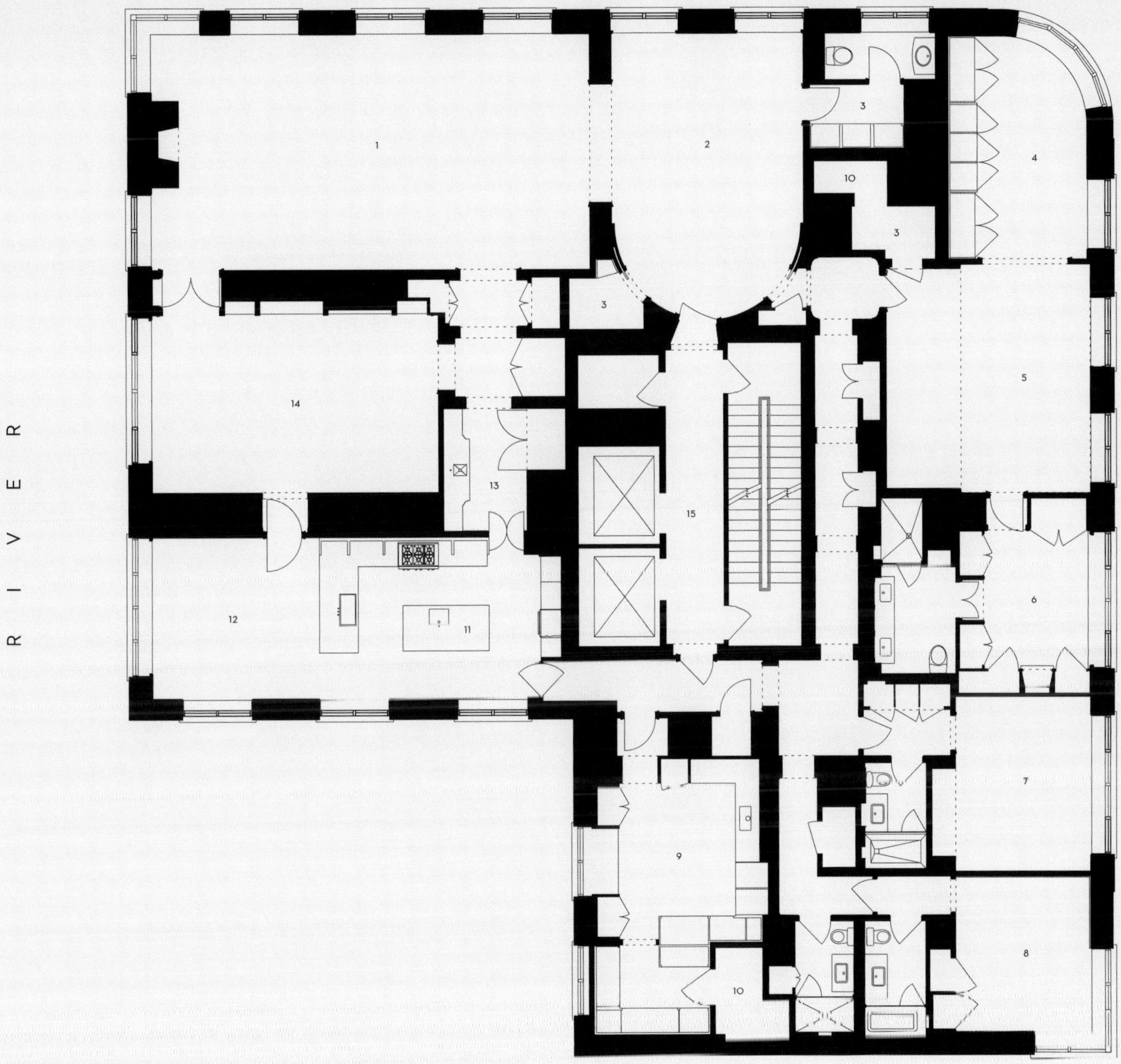

0 4 8 12 16 FT

COMPLETED FLOOR PLAN

1. LIVING ROOM
2. GALLERY
3. CLOAKROOM
4. SITTING ROOM
5. MASTER BEDROOM
6. DRESSING ROOM
7. BEDROOM
8. GYM
9. LAUNDRY ROOM
10. MECHANICAL ROOM
11. KITCHEN
12. BREAKFAST ROOM
13. BAR
14. DINING ROOM
15. ELEVATOR HALL

–

(Entrance Gallery), The entrance gallery captures the light and view while making space for a piano, and providing generous walls for art. The high gloss ceiling lends the impression of height.

BARBARA KASTEN: STAGES
HORST Photographer of Style
YAYOI KUSAMA GIVE ME LOVE
Jane Wilson Horizons

–

(Gallery into Living Room), A wide doorway creates an easy connection to the expanded living room.

–

(Living Room), While anchored by a fireplace, here the focus will always be the views out across the West Side and onto the Hudson River beyond.

PLAYBILL
AT THIS THEATRE
MICHELANGELO

We
Are No
Ourselve
THE ODYS
HOMER

–

Previous Spread, (Dining Room), The dining room is warm, with shelves, books, and a place to sit.

This Page, (Breakfast Table), The kitchen and breakfast table are awash in light.

(*Kitchen*), In redesigning the kitchen, we moved equipment off the wall to create a clear path along the windows.

–

(Dressing Room), The private realm is graced by light and soft surfaces.

–

(Personal Study), Off the master bedroom, in command of the building's curved corner window, is the owner's study.

–

Project drawing, Rita Marks
Project photography, Francesco Lagnese

PENTHOUSE APARTMENT

PARK AVENUE
NEW YORK

Of the eighty-one apartment buildings in New York designed by Rosario Candela, all of them still exist. His buildings are a crown jewel of New York's built endowment, and we count ourselves lucky when clients trust us with such an inheritance.

A Sicilian immigrant who arrived on Ellis Island in 1906, Candela rose with such confidence that while in graduate school at Columbia he would hang a velvet rope to block access to his drafting table, lest his peers nab his ideas. His first apartment house, in 1921, met with such success that by the end of 1922 Candela had designed seven more. This Park Avenue penthouse triplex dates from the late 1920s, the 'golden age' of Candela's output. Despite its provenance, it needed work and had been previously subjected to an unsympathetic alteration.

Not to say we started from a bad place. Candela had an ingenuity for tucking away all the practical parts of the building. To prevent intrusions on the plan, he thickened the exterior walls to house the building's structural steel as well as all the ducts and pipes. When it came time to vent all those pipes onto the roof, he would let them leap and tower through the flying arches and buttresses that make his rooftops so sculptural – culminating of course around water-towers, cloaked as soaring lanterns.

Like boatbuilders, we furthered that elegant efficiency. Everywhere, more fitted into less. Vents slipped into transoms, or – in the living room – a grille hid in plain sight, becoming a frame that followed the molding. Hardware companies supplied ingenious pocket doors and 'pull and pivot' paneling. A grid across the kitchen ceiling turned access panels into a thoughtful detail. To tie the whole home together, the entire staircase was rebuilt, coaxing more from each tread to minimize its footprint and pulling the stairs back to keep them from intruding into the foyer.

Working closely with the interior designer Jenny Fischbach, we took a rigorous approach to details, axes, frames, and doors throughout, to lend a sense of timelessness to our client's vision. It became a home with warmth, fun and just a little bit of whimsy.

For the plans, Candela pioneered the use of the entrance gallery as the access point for the apartment – it instantly orients the visitor. To establish rhythm and proportion, he would eschew doubling windows, having them instead march in regular succession. These plans were not stylistic straitjackets – for instance in 740 Park, even when brand new, Clarence Shearn's modern apartment co-existed with John D. Rockefeller Jr.'s Art Deco China rooms. Candela's plans are settings, perfect sites on which to create truly personal homes.

Movement depends as much upon differentiation as connection. Candela understood that, writing that "an ideal apartment, regardless of its size, must have its two or three sections, not infringing on each other, and easily connected to one another." In the 1920s, those sections were living, sleeping, and service. For this home, the sections were living, adults, and children. In the living area on the first floor, traditional service areas opened up to let the kitchen play a central role in the life of the apartment. The dining room adjoins it without the separation of a pantry, allowing it to function informally while, when needed, still able to dress up. For the adults, the second floor master suite links a master bedroom, well-appointed bath and a serene study. Finally, the children lay claim to the third floor, the penthouse, their space anchored by a spacious playroom adjacent to a purposefully retro kitchenette and diner booth tucked into a solarium and surrounded by terraces.

Rather than pull its inhabitants apart, differentiation between the parts of a home can, in fact, bring the family together. Indeed, in this home the children's section has proven the most popular. The mother loves best to work in the diner booth, while the children play nearby.

de Kooning

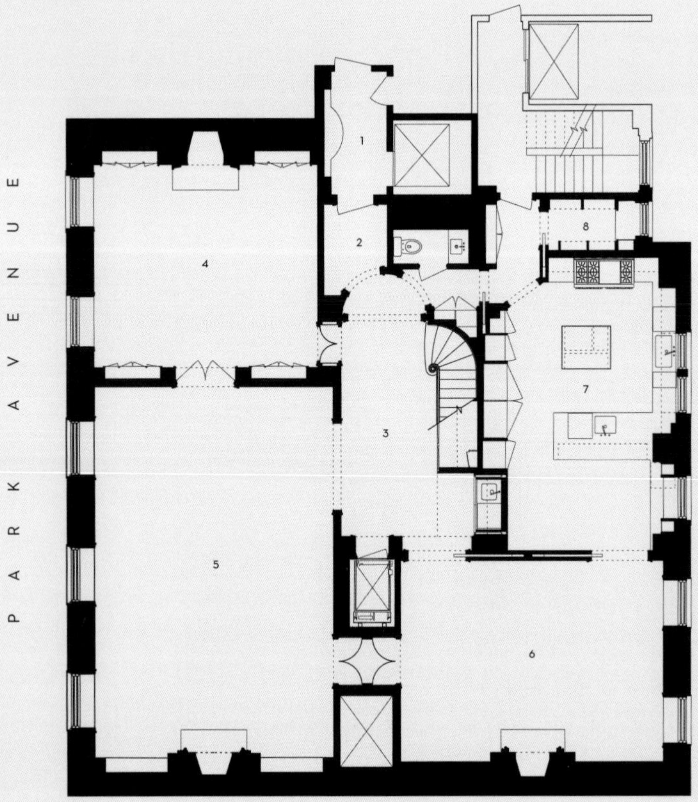

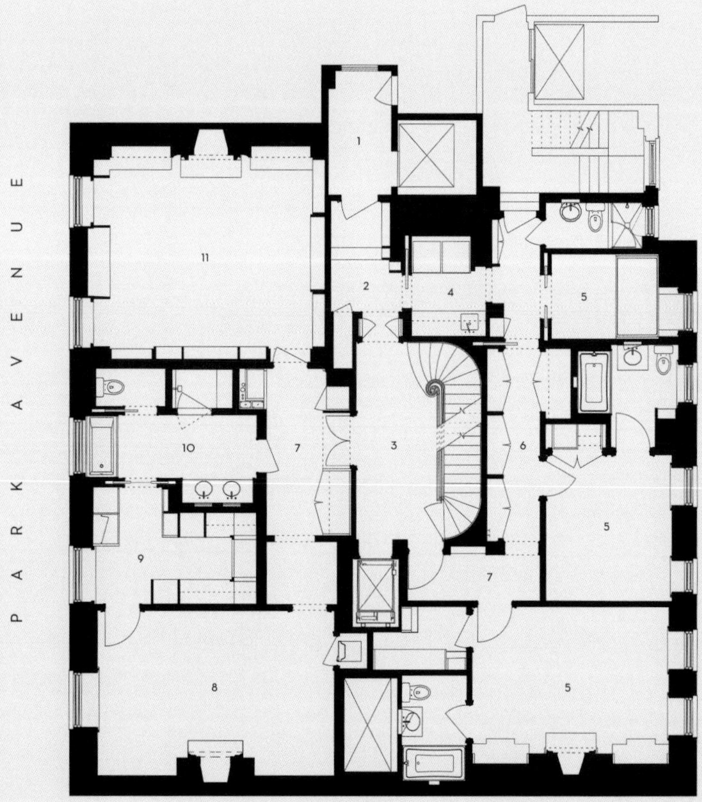

MAIN FLOOR PLAN

1. ELEVATOR HALL
2. FOYER
3. STAIR HALL
4. FAMILY ROOM
5. LIVING ROOM
6. DINING ROOM
7. KITCHEN
8. PANTRY

SECOND FLOOR PLAN

1. ELEVATOR HALL
2. MUD HALL
3. STAIR HALL
4. LAUNDRY
5. BEDROOM
6. CHILDREN'S HALL
7. HALL
8. MASTER BEDROOM
9. MASTER DRESSING ROOM
10. MASTER BATHROOM
11. MASTER STUDY

PENTHOUSE FLOOR PLAN

1. ELEVATOR HALL
2. PLAYROOM
3. BEDROOM
4. ROOF TERRACE
5. VESTIBULE
6. SOLARIUM
7. BAR

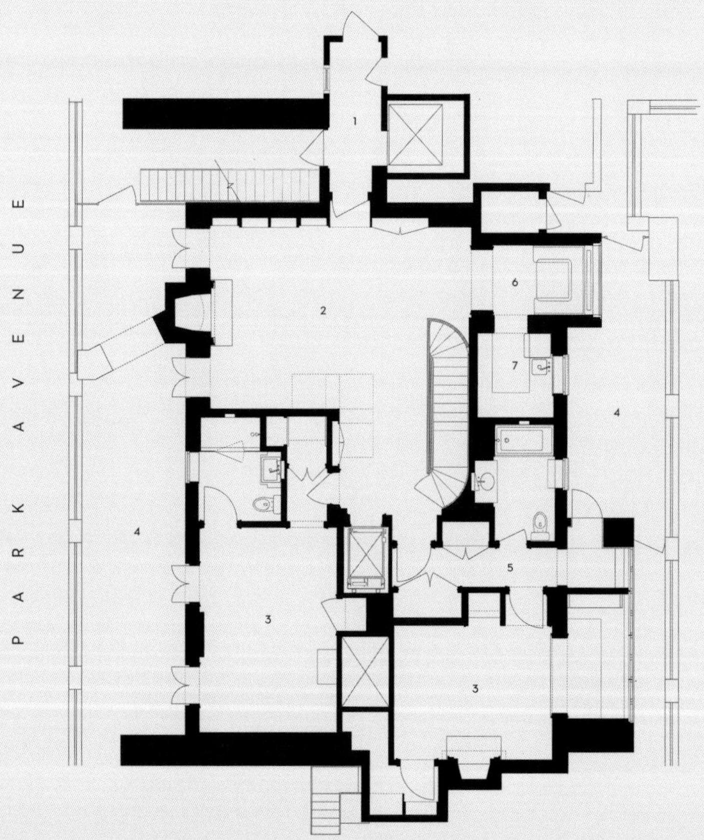

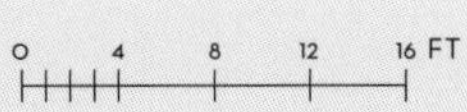

–

Spread 146-147, (Living Room), The living room's multiple doorways anchor the apartment.

Page 149, (Entrance Foyer), We rebuilt the entire staircase, coaxing more from each tread to pull the stairs back from the foyer about which the whole apartment turns.

–

Opposite, (Study), On the second floor, the study provides a place to work or relax.

This page, (Library), The library on the first-floor is a great sitting room.

–

(Master Bedroom), Blues help tie the home together.

–

(Master Bath), The stone on the walls of the bathroom echo the wood in the cabinets.

–

(Kitchen), The kitchen became an open, more stylish room, no longer service space, but a hub of the home's life.

–

(Dining). The kitchen's connection to the dining room allows it to function informally while still, in a pinch, able to dress up.

–

(Diner Booth). A purposefully retro kitchenette and diner booth tucked into a solarium has proven the home's most popular room. The mother loves best to work here, while the children play nearby.

–

Project drawing, Jairo Castro
Project photography, Durston Saylor

CARNEGIE HILL APARTMENT

UPPER EAST SIDE
NEW YORK

With every home the site is a primary consideration. The role of architecture is to organize and enhance what is already there, in as sympathetic a manner as possible. That said, for our firm many homes actually begin before the site. For this home, an apartment in Carnegie Hill, we were engaged by the family to look at different apartments, helping them choose the best one. When considering an apartment to purchase we look not just at the layout, but for potential, such as for how light and air can move through space, or whether we can forge more intimate connections between the parts of the home. We also guard against potential pitfalls, such as intrusive ductwork or other such necessary renovations – invisible upon inspection – that could impair the livability of the space.

Here, after a long search, our family chose an Emery Roth building. Emery Roth arrived in America as a thirteen year old orphan from Hungary with $7 in his pocket. With luck, scrap, and a romantic confidence in himself and his destiny, Roth found his footing in Chicago, where he worked in the office of Burnham and Root on the White City for the 1893 World's Fair. Upon opening his own practice in New York, he became one of the city's most prolific architects, counting in his portfolio masterpieces such as the San Remo, the Beresford, and the El Dorado. Along with fellow immigrant Rosario Candela and architects Schwartz & Gross and J.E.R. Carpenter, they would build the fabric of upper Manhattan. His buildings were spectacular, unique, and yet at one with their context. By his death he had designed more than two hundred and fifty of them.

He built apartments both disciplined by his classical training but imbued with the aspirations of the American dream he himself had realized. From a very practical standpoint, he was a pioneer – along with Rosario Candela – of the entrance foyer – the single room from which the rest of the apartment unfolds, in lieu of the long hallways that snaked through New York's early apartments.

While this was a gut renovation, given such good bones, we did not need to alter the apartment's configuration fundamentally. The focus could shift to more nuanced efforts. A clear axis ties together the main rooms, with thickened portals that in turn provided access to the rest of the apartment (while concealing hidden storage). The master and the daughter's bedrooms were swapped, leaving both more spacious. Our clients report the family room cozy and happy, comfortable from its proportion to its details. The family loves cooking socially, so we reworked what had been a service wing to open up the kitchen and connected it to a breakfast nook. One parent works from home, so we anchored the kitchen with a library and home office.

Tidiness and organization come not by expelling objects from the home, but simply from making a home for each object. In this apartment, that means we added many such homes, by way of a substantial number of closets, but in such a way that it brought rhythm and structure to the apartment, instead of being intrusive. The thickened walls and portals also provided more room to hide air handlers and ductwork. For that most dynamic collection of objects, clothes, our client tells us that the dressing room leaves her in awe of how organized her life has become.

Every design begins with the site, but every home begins with the client. Every client – everyone – should have the chance one day to design their own home. In this case, the client's young daughter arrived at our design meetings about as industrious and confident as Emery Roth once did in America. She came with a binder full of images and Instagram references. She would choose the color scheme and even cabinets for her room, and we believe her instincts proved sound.

Reference: *Mansions in the Clouds* by Steven Ruttenbaum, Foreword by Paul Goldberger, 1986.

EXISTING FLOOR PLAN

1. GALLERY
2. HALL
3. BEDROOM
4. CLOSET
5. LIBRARY
6. MASTER BEDROOM
7. LIVING ROOM
8. DINING ROOM
9. KITCHEN
10. STAFF ROOM
11. STUDY
12. SITTING ROOM

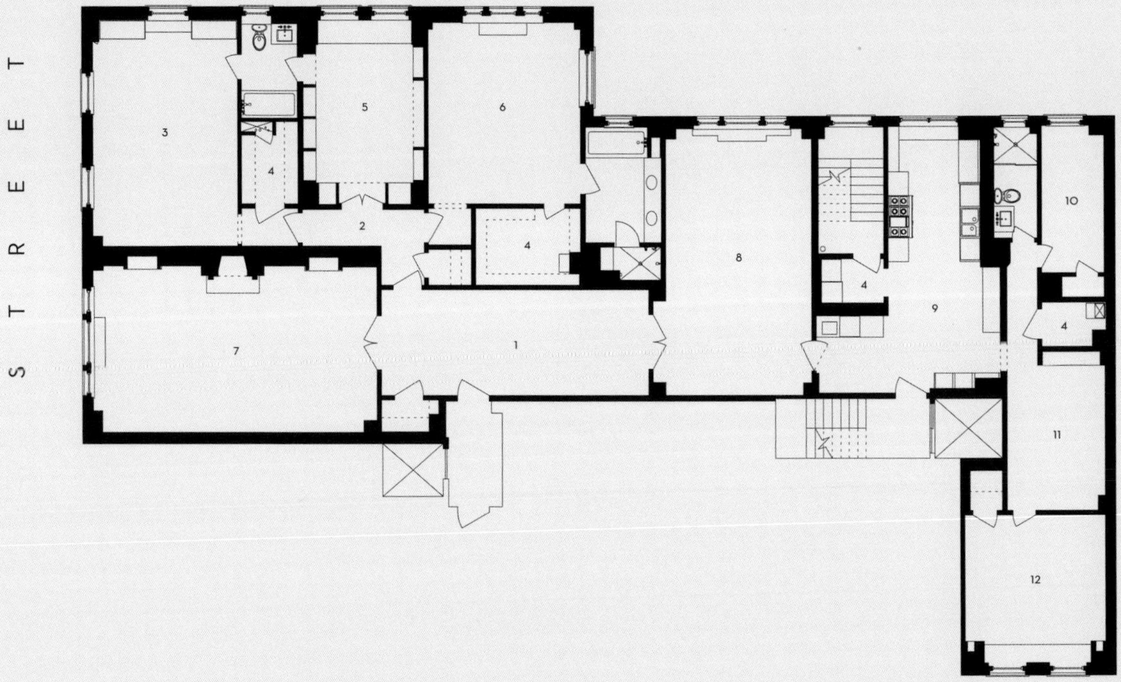

COMPLETED FLOOR PLAN

1. ENTRY GALLERY
2. HALL
3. BEDROOM
4. HER DRESSING ROOM
5. MASTER BEDROOM
6. HIS DRESSING ROOM
7. LIVING ROOM
8. DINING ROOM
9. BUTLER'S PANTRY
10. KITCHEN
11. BREAKFAST NOOK
12. LAUNDRY
13. STUDY
14. FAMILY ROOM

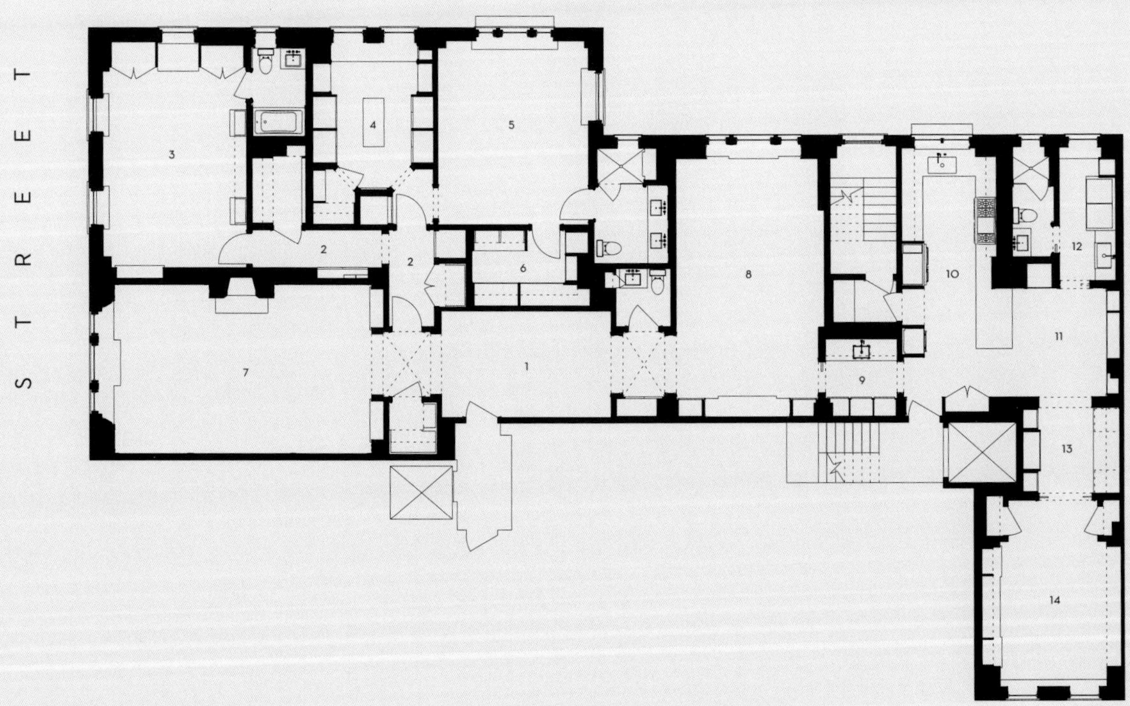

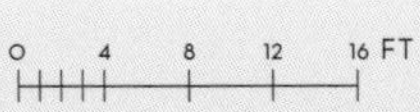

ART AND LOVE IN
RENAISSANCE ITALY
MIRÓ

–

Page 161, (Entrance Gallery), The gallery ties the main rooms together through deep paneled doorways.

Spread 162-163, (Living Room), For social events, the gallery is flanked by a large living room on one side and the dining room on the other, so the flow for the guests is easy and welcoming.

–

Opposite, (Entrance Hall), Across the doorway from the living room is the dining room. The simple and strong pattern in the polished stone floor defines space and transition.

This Page, (Dining Room), The sideboard, integrated into the dining room and referencing classic antecedents, provides ample storage coupled with an elegant design.

SUB-ZERO
HORIZON
ORGANIC
LOWFAT
MILK

–

(Kitchen), The family loves cooking socially, so we reworked what had been a service wing to open up the kitchen and connected it to a breakfast nook.

This Page, (Breakfast Nook and Home Office), The kitchen opens to a breakfast room nook with hidden storage and a home office beyond.

Opposite, *(Pantry)*, A pantry area was created between the dining room and kitchen.

–

(Daughter's Room), The client's daughter arrived at our design meetings with a binder full of images and Instagram references. She would choose the color scheme and even cabinets for her room, and we believe her instincts proved sound.

–

Project drawing, Olivia Rowan
Project photography, Durston Saylor

Harry Potter

TOWNHOUSES

Townhouse renovations require both the humility to match the most exacting constraints and the confidence to build and imagine from scratch.

Take for example a Lenox Hill project. The building came as a timeless neighborhood gem, with a façade and parlor floor by the firm Walker & Gillette. A later renovation, however, punched a storefront into its front. A suitable entrance needed to be composed. Embracing the landmarks review process, we drew and worked through almost a dozen different options before arriving on a solution that worked. A sturdy door nestles under a deep and gently pointed arch. It pairs with a window that adopts the black mullions and quoined limestone frame from the upper floors. For our back elevation, we continued to channel Walker & Gillette. We composed a double bay window in limestone, set on a brick wall.

So much for the humility. The entire interior of the house had been through serial renovations that chopped it up into small parts. We ripped all of it out, put a new steel frame in, and reworked the full six floors as a house that fit the needs of our client. The parlor floor was moved upward a foot to give the living spaces in the ground floor a little more headroom. A spacious kitchen ties together the ground floor and enjoys the light and views of the courtyard at the rear. A new formal stair brings the guest from the entry to the living room on the parlor floor. The upper floors accommodate the usual program of bedrooms, baths, and storage, all composed to allow furniture to be placed effortlessly and building systems to be concealed. One is never reminded of the constraints of planning between parallel walls.

The same balance of care and confidence defined a townhouse project in Carnegie Hill done with decorator Delphine Krakoff. It was important to the neighborhood that the historic front elevation stay almost exactly intact. The back elevation was a different story. An awkward addition was removed.

In its place, we built a new double height window for the ground and parlor floors, with a two-storey bay window on top. The interior changed even more radically. The townhouse is so close to Central Park that it was built on debris removed to create the Park, making the foundation unstable. To improve matters, the structural engineers at Silman helped insert a new steel frame into the house's walls, allowing the creation of spaces that could precisely relate to one another, unimpeded by vestigial load bearing elements. The steel provided the framework to take a building originally partitioned into small apartments and transform it into a single-family home.

The heart of that home is a sculptural stair, 'floated' as a single piece of plaster. The stair's landings organize the home, from a roof garden on top, to a playroom anchoring the children's floor, to a dining room on the mezzanine overlooking the living room and the garden beyond, and finally – at its ground floor culmination – the combined kitchen and double height living room. A double storey bay window with a green wall holds spaces for retreat, with two rooms for the children, and a master bathroom for the parents.

Sometimes the disconnect between façade and interior is even more complete, such as when a family had bought two townhouses on the Upper West Side. The neighborhood wanted their front façade to appear as two distinct townhouses. The family wanted to enjoy the full width of the two combined townhouses. So we cleared the interior for a series of rooms spanning the entire width, while carefully restoring the brownstone detail on the front.

By this point, the game across the more than a dozen townhouses we have renovated should be clear. The two side walls remain sacred, and the front elevation almost always remains the same. Within and behind, however, everything is possible.

Project drawing, Rita Marks

VARIATIONS ON A THEME

AN IMAGINARY STREET

–

This composition of the main floors on twelve different townhouse renovations, all by Oliver Cope Architect, demonstrates the vast number of possibilities for any townhouse.

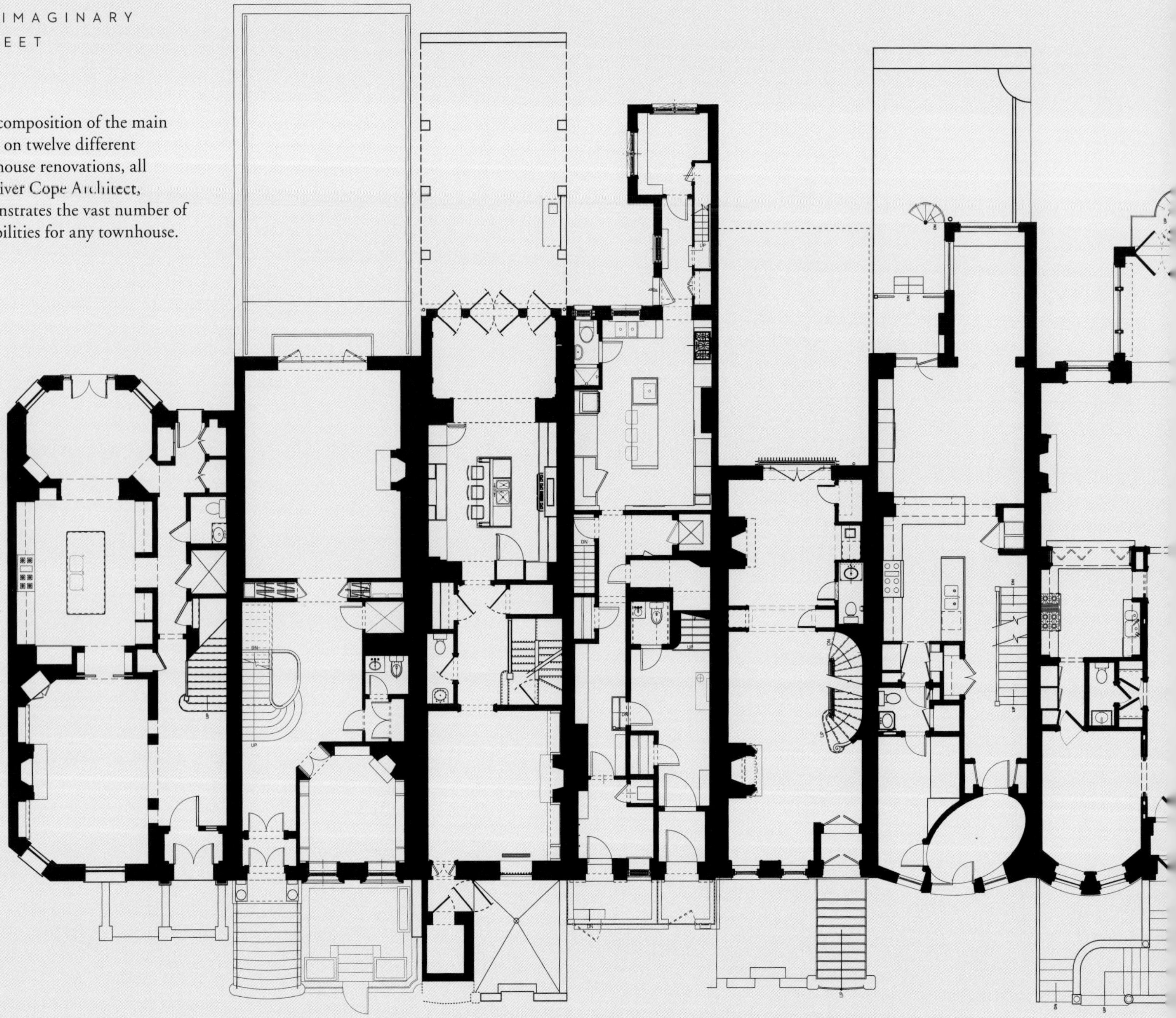

West 91st Street	East 74th Street	West 84th Street	East 70th Street	East 69th Street	West 88th Street	West 87t Street

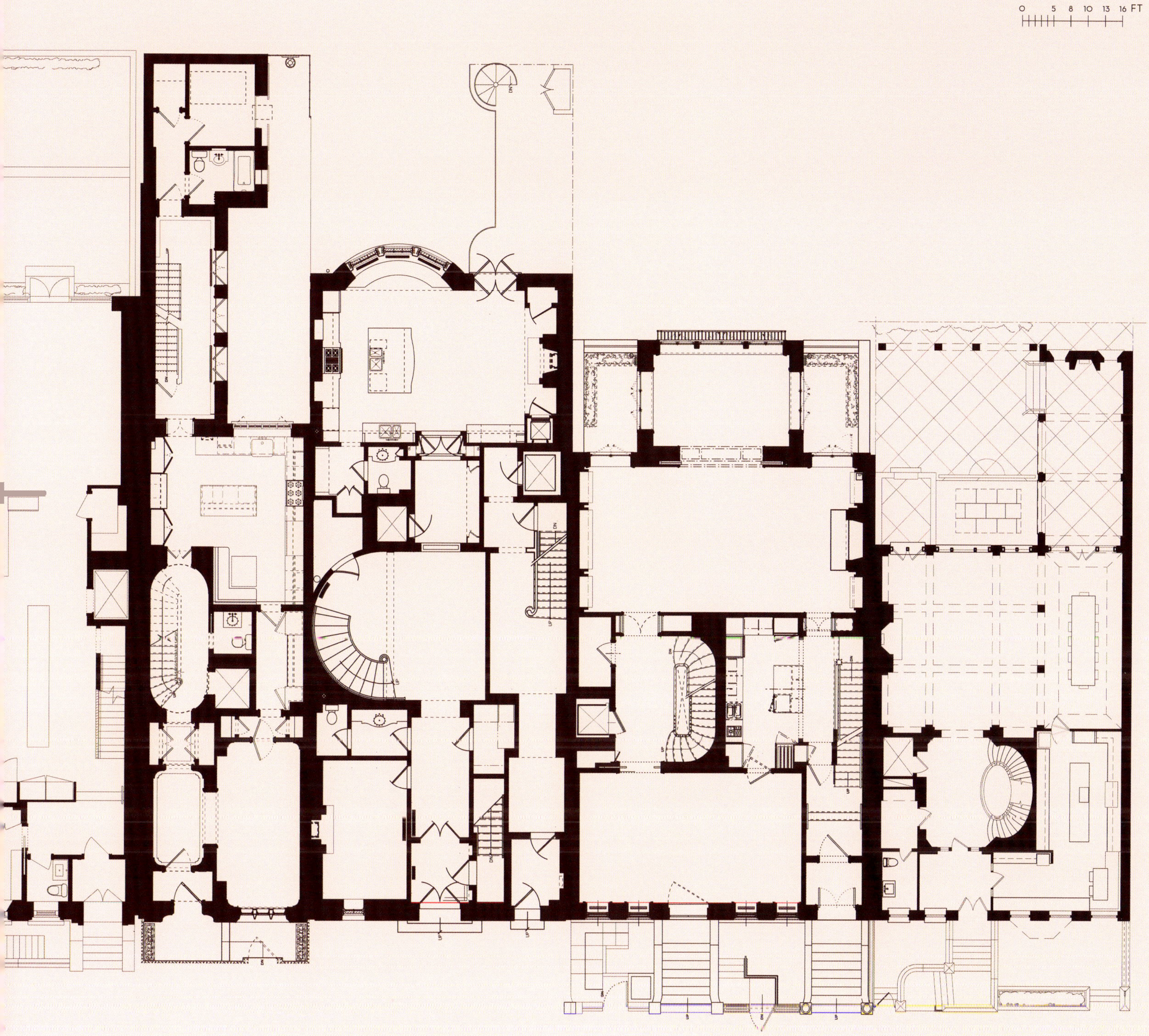

East 93rd Street

East 70th Street

East 69th Street

West 83rd Street

West 69th Street

E. 70TH ST.

This townhouse came as a timeless neighborhood gem, with a façade and parlor floor by the firm Walker & Gillette. A later renovation, however, punched a storefront into its front. A suitable entrance needed to be composed. Embracing the landmarks review process, we drew and worked through almost a dozen different options before arriving on a solution that worked. For our back elevation, we continued to channel Walker & Gillette. We composed a double bay window in limestone, set on a brick wall.

The townhouse benefitted additionally from a strategic decision regarding the front stairs. They would only run from the ground floor to the formal rooms on the parlor floor. The stairs in the back would provide service to the rest of the house. Such a strategic discipline allowed the rest of the home the increased flexibility to fit the various closets, baths, and bedrooms a family needs, all while enjoying the full width of the townhouse, uncompromised by a set of stairs.

–

(Front Elevation), Reinventing and restoring a façade, into which a Depression era storefront had been inserted required invention within context.

–

Project photography, Chuck Choi

1. STAIR HALL
2. ELEVATOR

1. STAIR HALL
2. ELEVATOR
3. ENTRY
4. ENTRY HALL
5. DINING ROOM
6. BUTLER'S PANTRY
7. KITCHEN
8. BEDROOM
9. GARDEN
10. LIVING ROOM
11. BAR
12. OFFICE
13. FAMILY ROOM
14. HIS STUDY
15. HALL
16. CLOSET

1. STAIR HALL
2. ELEVATOR
3. BEDROOM
4. GYM
5. MASTER BEDROOM
6. HER DRESSING ROOM
7. HIS DRESSING ROOM
8. MASTER BATHROOM
9. ROOF DECK
10. LINEN HALL
11. LAUNDRY ROOM
12. PLAY ROOM

–

(Stairs), The front stairs only run from the ground floor to the formal rooms on the parlor floor.

–

(Pantry), A carefully detailed butler's pantry connects the kitchen to the dining room.

UPPER WEST SIDE

W. 84TH ST.

This home benefitted from an exceptionally deep backyard. The challenge was how to use that depth without cutting even more precious light away from the townhouse itself. The solution arrived upon was to add a conservatory. It provided a spacious room for dining, while its glass walls drew more light into the kitchen and interior beyond. The same strategy applied above, where the addition of two bay windows increased the total amount of windows on each of the upper floors, while creating rooms with personality and light.

–

(Office), Even a home that focuses on the light should still have a place of warmth and retreat – here the office plays that role.

–

Project photography, Durston Saylor

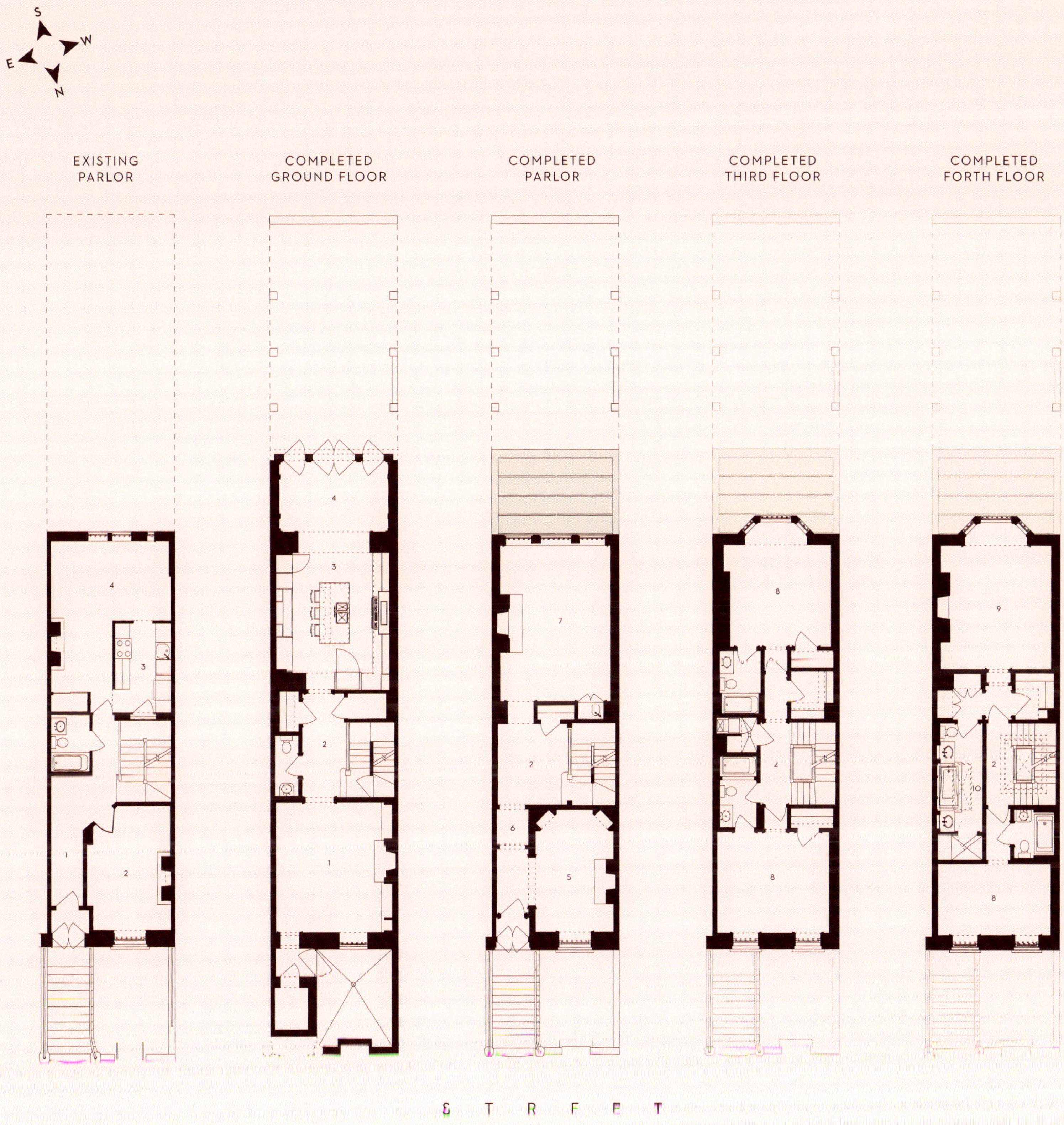

1. HALL
2. RECEPTION ROOM
3. KITCHEN
4. DINING ROOM

1. FAMILY ROOM
2. STAIR HALL
3. KITCHEN
4. DINING
5. STUDY

6. ENTRY HALL
7. LIVING ROOM
8. BEDROOM
9. MASTER BEDROOM
10. MASTER BATHROOM

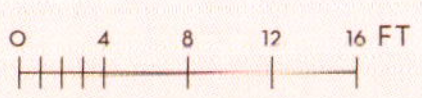

–

(Dining Room), The dining table enjoys the light of the conservatory, which spills into the kitchen beyond.

–

(Back Yard), The home's exceptionally deep backyard allowed both the addition of the conservatory as well as two bay windows, above.

CARNEGIE HILL

E. 93RD ST.

This townhouse, organized around its mezzanines, began as a building of five flats, each floor its own unit. The practical and thoughtful elevations of the architects, by A.B. Ogden & Son, established the scale and character of the neighborhood. In the 1930s, the composer and song writer Irving Berlin bought the building, and though he never moved in, he renovated it to fit ten units, splitting each of the original five in half, and adding a fire escape to the front. One of only a few A.B. Ogden & Son buildings now left, it was important to the neighborhood that we keep the elevation almost exactly intact. As we were taking a building with ten units and turning it into a home for a single family, almost everything else changed. In fact, working with the decorator Delphine Krakoff, we essentially created a new building.

Reference: *Carnegie Hill Expanded Historic District,* New York City Landmarks Preservation Commission, Dec. 21, 1993.

–

(Stair), We believe stairs are as much sculpture as simple vertical circulation.

–

Project photography, Devon Banks

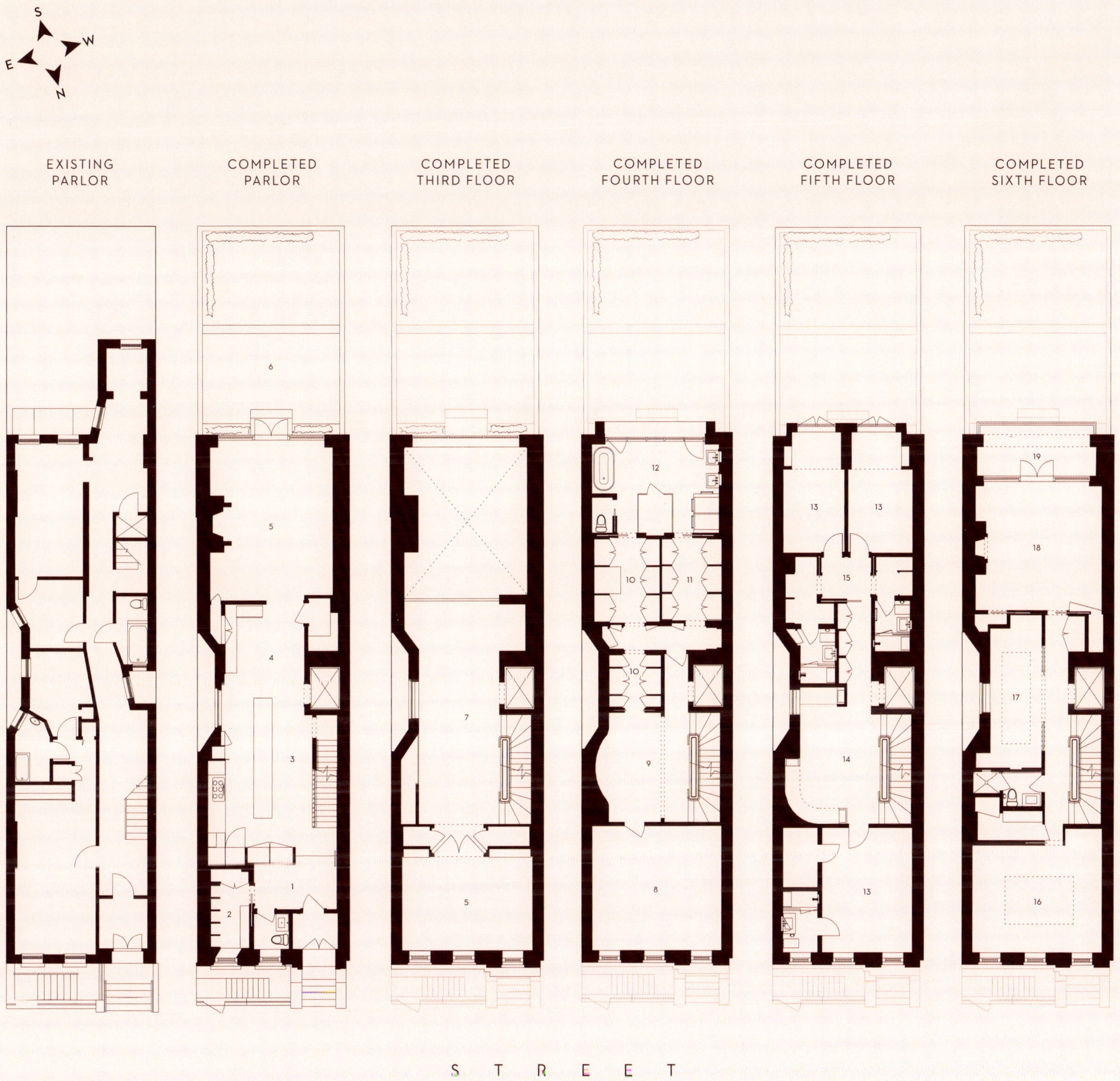

1. ENTRY VESTIBULE
2. MUDROOM
3. KITCHEN
4. BREAKFAST ROOM
5. LIVING ROOM
6. REAR GARDEN
7. DINING ROOM
8. MASTER BEDROOM
9. STAIR HALL
10. HER DRESSING ROOM
11. HIS DRESSING ROOM
12. MASTER BATHROOM
13. BEDROOM
14. CHILDREN'S LOUNGE
15. VESTIBULE
16. RECREATION ROOM
17. GYM
18. STUDY
19. EXTERIOR TERRACE

0 4 8 12 16 FT

–

(Living Room), Removing a portion of the second floor and the rear extension sacrificed floor area to gain so much more.

–

(Bath), The master bath is in a bay window covered in ivy, permitting privacy and a full wall of light.

UPPER WEST SIDE COMBINATION

WEST. 83RD ST.

Here the façade and interior are completely different. A family had bought two townhouses on the Upper West Side and wanted our help combining them. It was important to the neighborhood that their front façade be so well preserved that they continue to appear as two distinct townhouses. It was important to the family that they enjoy the full width of the two combined townhouses. So we opened up a series of rooms that spanned the entire width, while not touching the front elevations. The family hosts large gatherings for the holidays, so the largest spaces were the places of gathering – the kitchen, the dining room, and the living room. For the kitchen in particular, the family wanted a place where the whole home came together. On the ground floor, that kitchen connects smoothly to a dining table, a family nook, a home office, and a basketball court in the combined backyard.

–

(Stairs), Here just 14", the gap between the treads and the landings allows light to dance down through the whole house.

–

Project photography, Devon Banks

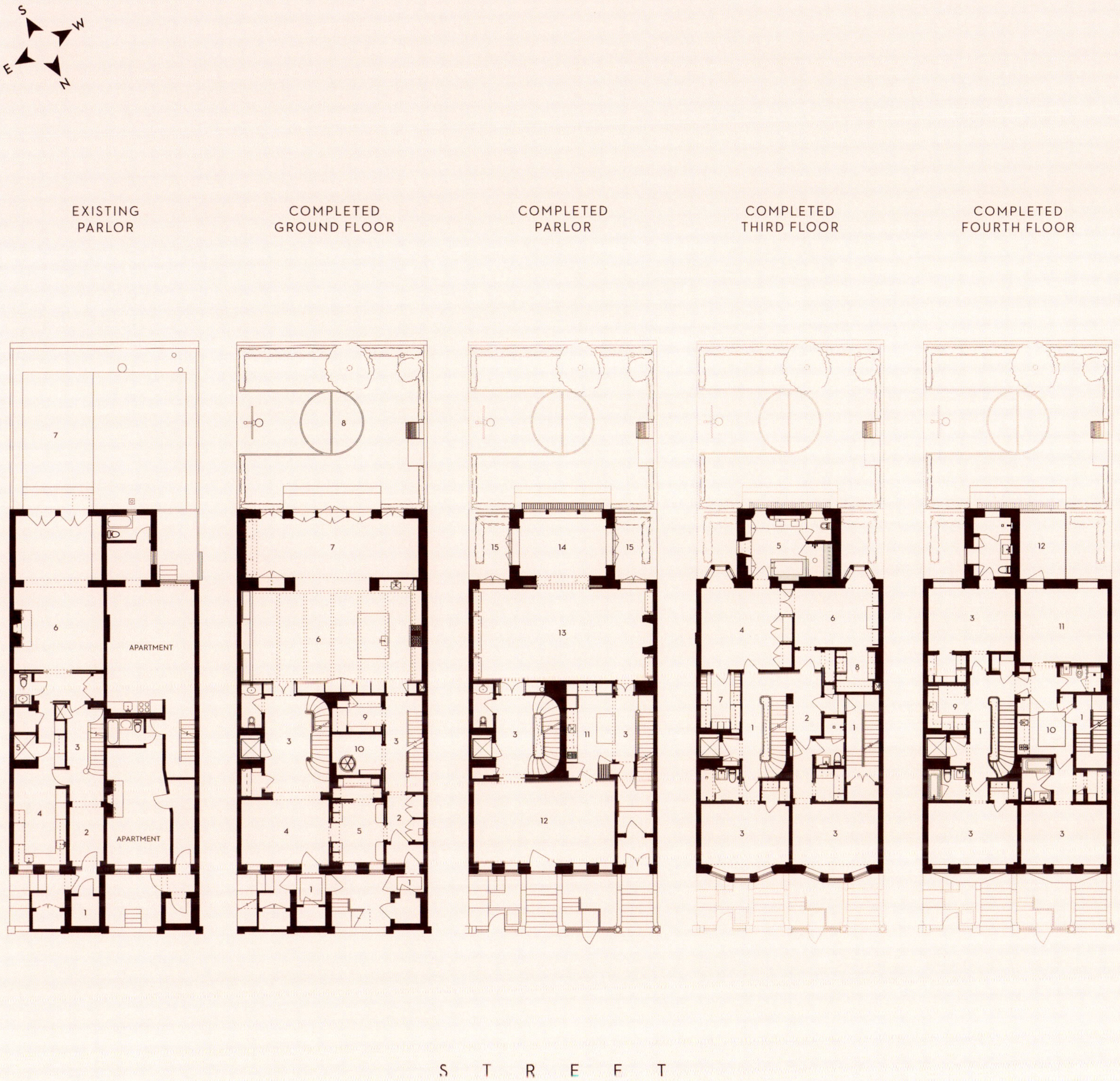

1. STORAGE
2. ENTRY
3. STAIR HALL
4. KITCHEN
5. ELEVATOR
6. LIVING ROOM
7. REAR GARDEN

1. UNDERSTOOP
2. HALL
3. STAIR HALL
4. ENTRY
5. MUDROOM
6. KITCHEN
7. FAMILY ROOM
8. REAR GARDEN
9. PANTRY
10. BIKE STORAGE
11. BUTLER'S PANTRY
12. DINING ROOM
13. LIVING ROOM
14. SUN ROOM
15. TERRACE

1. STAIR HALL
2. HALL
3. BEDROOM
4. MASTER BEDROOM
5. MASTER BATHROOM
6. STUDY
7. HER CLOSET
8. HIS CLOSET
9. LAUNDRY
10. KITCHENETTE
11. LIVING ROOM
12. TERRACE

0 4 8 12 16 FT

–

(Kitchen), The family wanted to bring all parts of the home together around the kitchen, including a dining table, a seating cluster, and a home office, all opening up onto the backyard.

–

(Living Room), Spaces spanning the full double width of the combined townhouse allowed for rooms with generous and relaxed compositions, such as here, with the pool table.

SEA

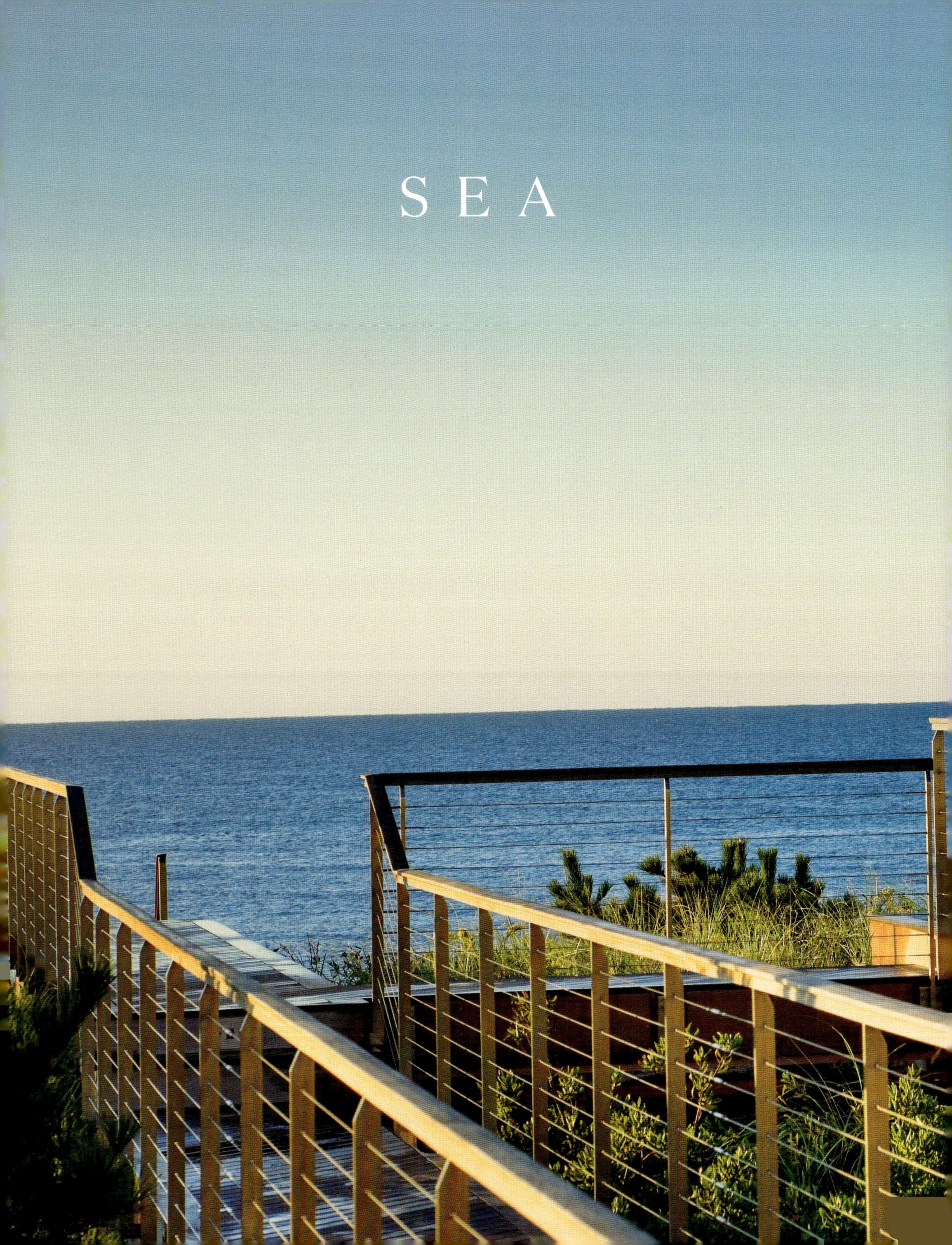

SHINGLE HOUSE

COVE NECK
LONG ISLAND

The program for this home contained a contradiction. We had to design a seaside home as both a refuge for the parents and playground for the children. How can a home be both peaceful and playful? Fortunately, the northeast holds a vernacular perfectly suited for such a challenge, the Shingle Style.

Pioneered in the 1880s by H.H. Richardson and his protégés Charles McKim and Stanford White (of the firm McKim, Mead & White), the Shingle Style took hold so quickly and organically because – in the words of the historian Vincent Scully – it tapped into America's intellectual pluralism, "wherein many divergent attitudes and influences are supposed to merge into an integrated but not 'exclusive' whole." How does that work? Stretched across a timber frame, all of those shingles – on the roofs, on the walls, and even emulated in details like densely mullioned windows – give the envelope of a home a coherence that allows its actual massing to possess a great deal of variety. All of that flexibility allows for a home both coherent and unique, one that allows for programmatic necessities to be expressed artistically and compositionally in the house as a whole.

The form of this home comes from its site, which is a low-lying point extending into Long Island Sound. Its half-butterfly plan hugs the driveway and captures the southern light, while opening up to the views out across Long Island Sound to the north. Two towers anchor the home and aptly symbolize the contradictions it contains. The tower overlooking the driveway and garage holds a spiral stairway culminating in an outdoor playroom. The tower with the most privacy, in command of views of the sea, holds a peaceful sunroom – accessible only from the master bedroom. The interior builds on the relationship between those two towers. One side of the house contains informal spaces, such as the family room, the breakfast room, and the kitchen.

A covered walkway provides access to the garage, and the pool sits neatly off the family room. The opposite wing holds the living and dining rooms – spaces in which the parents can entertain while at a safe remove from the melee beyond.

The home is for the extended family, which posed a special problem for bedrooms. The math of a two-storey house means, more or less, that the area of the second floor, that is the area of the bedrooms, has to be equal to the area of the first floor, that is the rest of the rooms. To allow for more room on the second floor than was needed below, we wrapped almost the entire first floor in a porch. While keeping rooms downstairs slim and full of light and air, we made an upstairs with plenty of room for the bedrooms, bathrooms, and closets that a large family needs. The whole home comes together in its front hall. The upstairs and the downstairs, the inside and outside, the formal rooms and the informal rooms all cross paths here.

Every project has surprises long after the plans are approved. This home offered a happy one on top, that started with necessary safety measure on the bottom. Flooding is a real danger, and local regulations required new structures to be raised sixteen feet above sea level – six feet above existing grade. The house therefore has a steel frame, sitting on a concrete cap, laid atop deeply driven wooden piles. A combination of fill and stone cladding disguises this podium. The surprise came on the consequently very high roof, where a meeting of the house's gambrel and gabled masses left a flat triangular patch on top of the house, adjacent to its cupola. The owners were so taken with the view, that we changed the plans to build a railing around it and a special stair for access. From this improvised crow's nest, Long Island Sound, marshes, and ponds are visible on all three sides, ever changing with the tide's advance and retreat.

FIRST FLOOR PLAN

1. LIVING ROOM
2. BAR
3. LIBRARY
4. HALL
5. ENTRY/STAIR HALL
6. PORCH
7. MECHANICAL ROOM
8. DINING ROOM
9. PANTRY
10. FOYER
11. STAIR HALL
12. KITCHEN
13. BREAKFAST ROOM
14. SCREENED PORCH
15. FAMILY ROOM
16. MUDROOM
17. PLAYROOM
18. LAUNDRY
19. MECHANICAL DECK
20. TOWER STAIR HALL
21. WALKWAY
22. GARAGE STAIR HALL
23. GARAGE
24. STORAGE
25. REFUSE

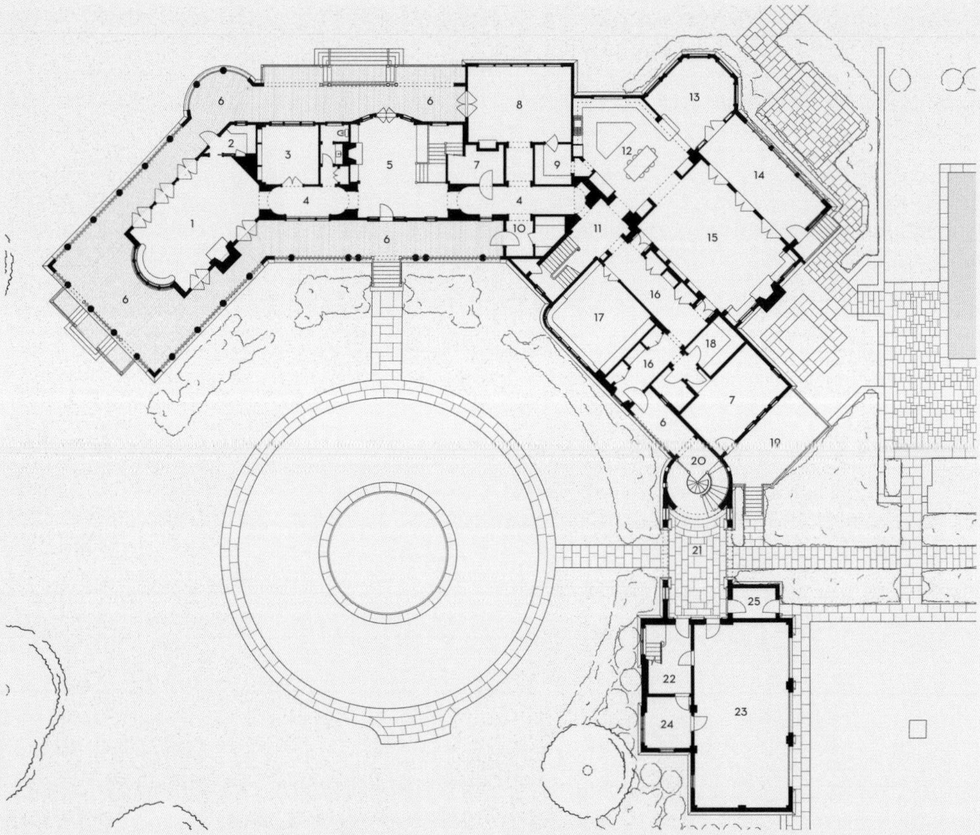

SECOND FLOOR PLAN

1. GYM
2. DRESSING ROOM
3. HALL
4. MASTER BEDROOM
5. SITTING ROOM
6. BALCONY
7. BEDROOM
8. OFFICE
9. STAIR HALL
10. STORAGE
11. TOWER

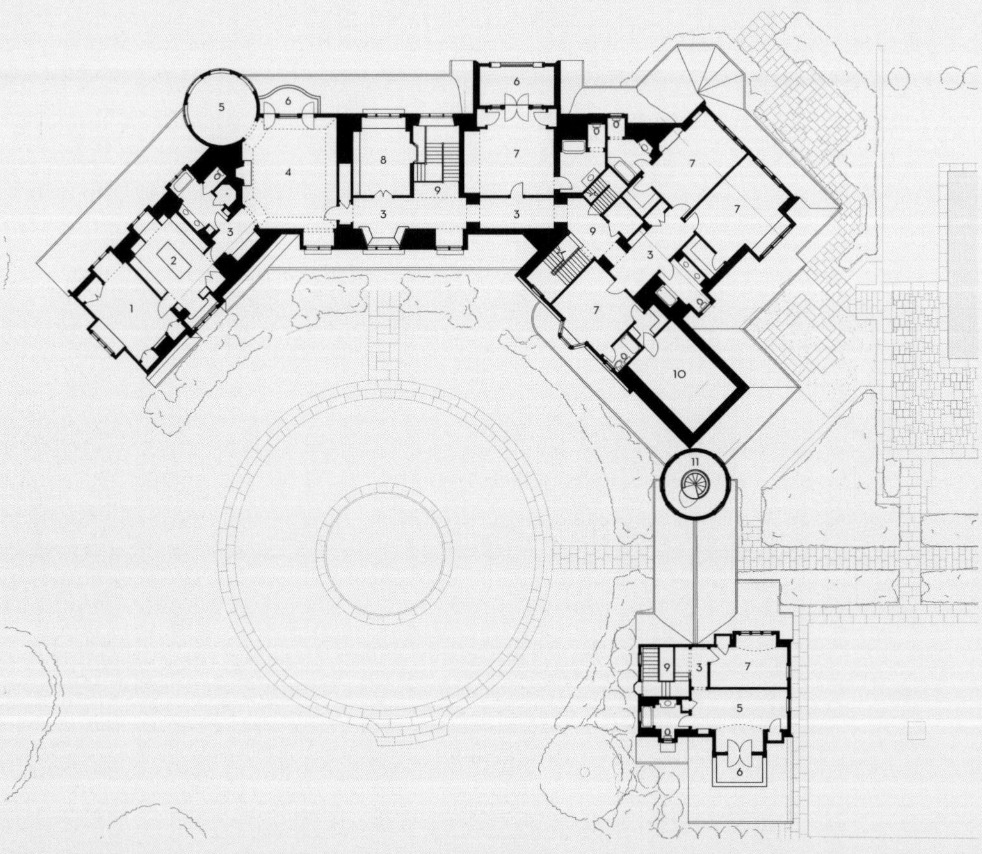

0 4 8 12 16 FT

Page 197, (Living Room Porch & Garage), Shingle Style, named after all of those shingles – on the roofs, on the walls, and even emulated in details like densely mullioned windows – gives the envelope of a home a coherence that allows its actual massing to possess a great deal of variety.

Spread 198-199, (South Side), The form of this home comes from its site, which is a low-lying point extending into Long Island Sound. Two towers anchor the home. The one overlooking the driveway and garage holds a spiral stairway culminating in an outdoor playroom.

Opposite, (Tower), The tower with the most privacy, in command of views of the sea, holds a sunroom accessible only from the master bedroom.

This page, (West Side), To allow for more room on the second floor than was needed below, we wrapped almost the entire first floor with a porch.

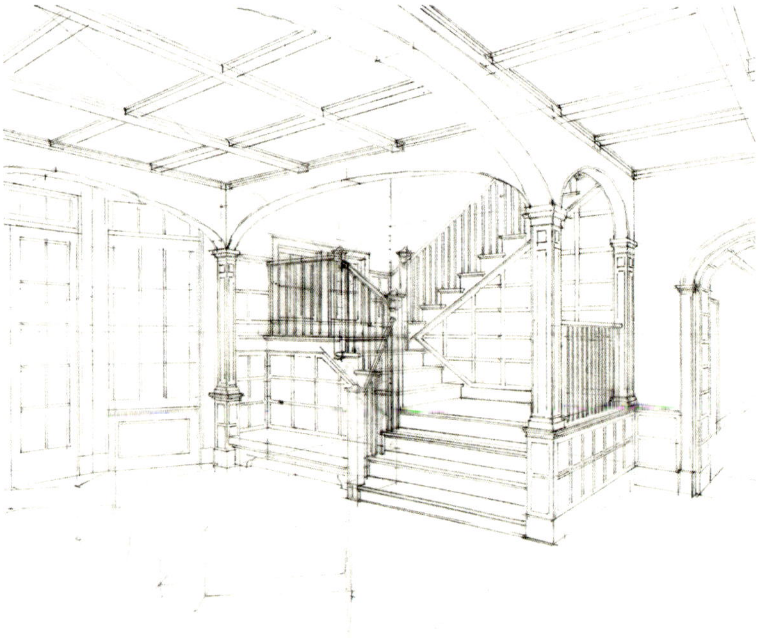

1.

PROCESS.

The classic Shingle Style house is known not just for its shingled exterior, but for the stair hall that traditionally was as much a place for living as for circulation through the house. Starting from design precedents by Henry Hobson Richardson and Stanford White, we used built-in benches, a fireplace and warm woods to make a space that is both elegant and comfortable. An interior bay window peers over the space from above.

2.

3.

4.

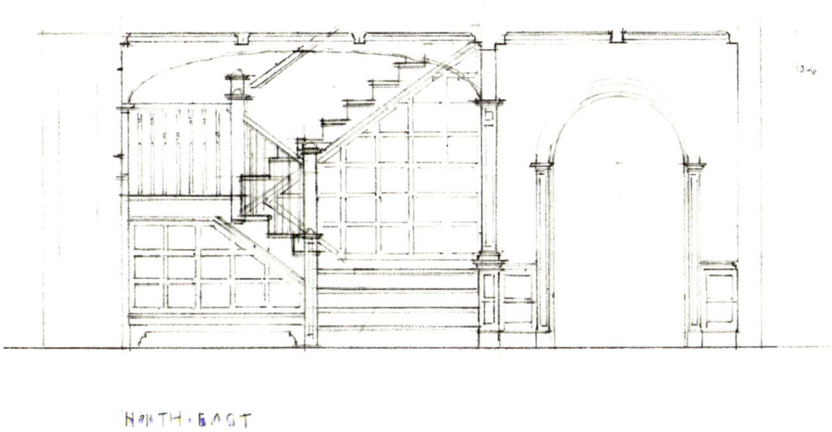

4.

1. PERSPECTIVE SKETCH
2. TOWARDS LIVING ROOM
3. UP THE STAIRS
4. ELEVATIONS

–

(Kitchen), One side of the house contains informal spaces, such as the family room, the breakfast room, and the kitchen.

–

(Family Room), We believe every home deserves an inglenook.

–

(Living Room), By keeping the first floor narrow, we filled it with light and air.

–

Project drawing, Morgen Fleisig
Project photography, Chuck Choi

A NORMAN HOUSE

CENTRE ISLAND
LONG ISLAND

How do you build a home around the sunset? This property began with a house on it. It was a grand and historic Long Island estate, but it did not work. There were no porches, and its rooms suffered from a complete disconnect to the view. A misbegotten renovation from shingle to stucco Georgian had further confused matters. The site, in the meantime, was magnificent. Tree studded lawns sweep into the Long Island Sound. A fringe of interior woodland provided safety and a real sense of depth. The client wanted a home in harmony with this context. When *House & Garden* later featured it, they noted that while harmony and ease in a garden usually only come with the work of time – usually decades – after only three years the new home's gardens already looked deeply settled and radiant.

How did we do it? The new home puts a series of external rooms into relationships with one another and the land. Those rooms range from the front drive to a formal garden. For strategy we drew on a French precedent, the *hôtel particulier*. Not at all a hotel, the term refers to a type of house that proliferated in 18th century Paris. As the city grew prosperous, the newly wealthy wedged ever grander houses into its medieval pre-Haussmann plan. Like the British Tudor house, they were opportunistic, turning every bit of their assembled plots, no matter how irregular, into useful space. Yet in contrast to the Tudor, they did not celebrate their quirkiness. Instead, like chameleons, a *hôtel particulier* would adopt clear geometries from its context. Together with the city, a *hôtel particulier* would form magnificent exterior squares, and put them into relationship to equally awesome interior courts.

The most fundamental relationship of our home is between the formal drive and the

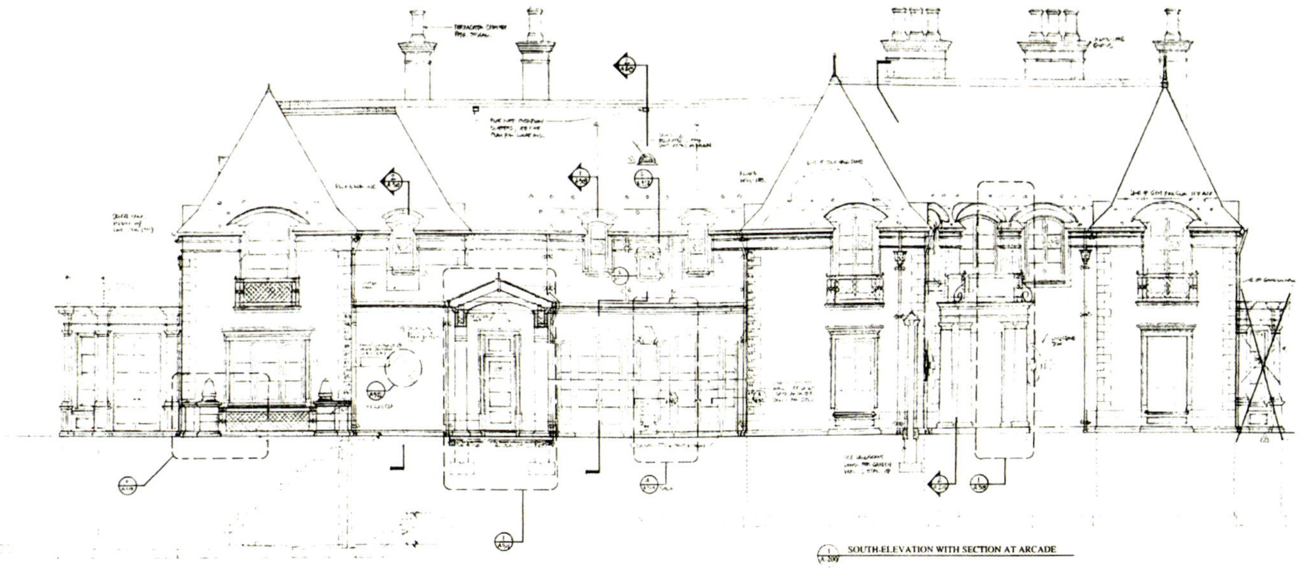

house's culmination, an arced terrace and lawn overlooking the sound and the sunset. The space between the two becomes the front hall, with both a direct visual access to car and the sound, and the axis off of which the rest of the rooms develop. The entertaining rooms – dining and living – open directly off the front. We believe in houses that are used, in their entirety, every day, so lest the living room sit unused outside of major events, we tucked a library and office just beyond it. Beyond the dining room – in a space defined by the car park and the pool and its decks – are the kitchen and family rooms. The family did not want to eat in the kitchen, so we set aside an adjacent but separate breakfast room. We also do not believe in back doors as after thoughts, so we made the door coming off the garage to the kitchen special, by binding the garage to the kitchen with an arcade. We wove the site and home together with doors and loggias, including one from the family room onto the pergola, one from the front hall, dining room and living room onto the terrace, and even one from the library onto the back garden. This house would be an excellent one for hide-and-seek.

We did convince the client to keep intact one vestige of the old house, the allée of Linden trees that had been its front drive. It no longer made sense as a front drive, so on the advice of our collaborator, the landscape architect Peter Cummin, we simply moved the drive over. Like a ruin, two towers embrace the end of the allée – they are in fact the mechanical room of the garage, and a poolside shower large enough to knock the chlorine out of the hair of a whole litter of small children. Above and on axis to the trees is a daughter's bedroom, its window in command of a regal row of Lindens beyond. Between them, Peter had planted violets, creating a carpet of blue each spring.

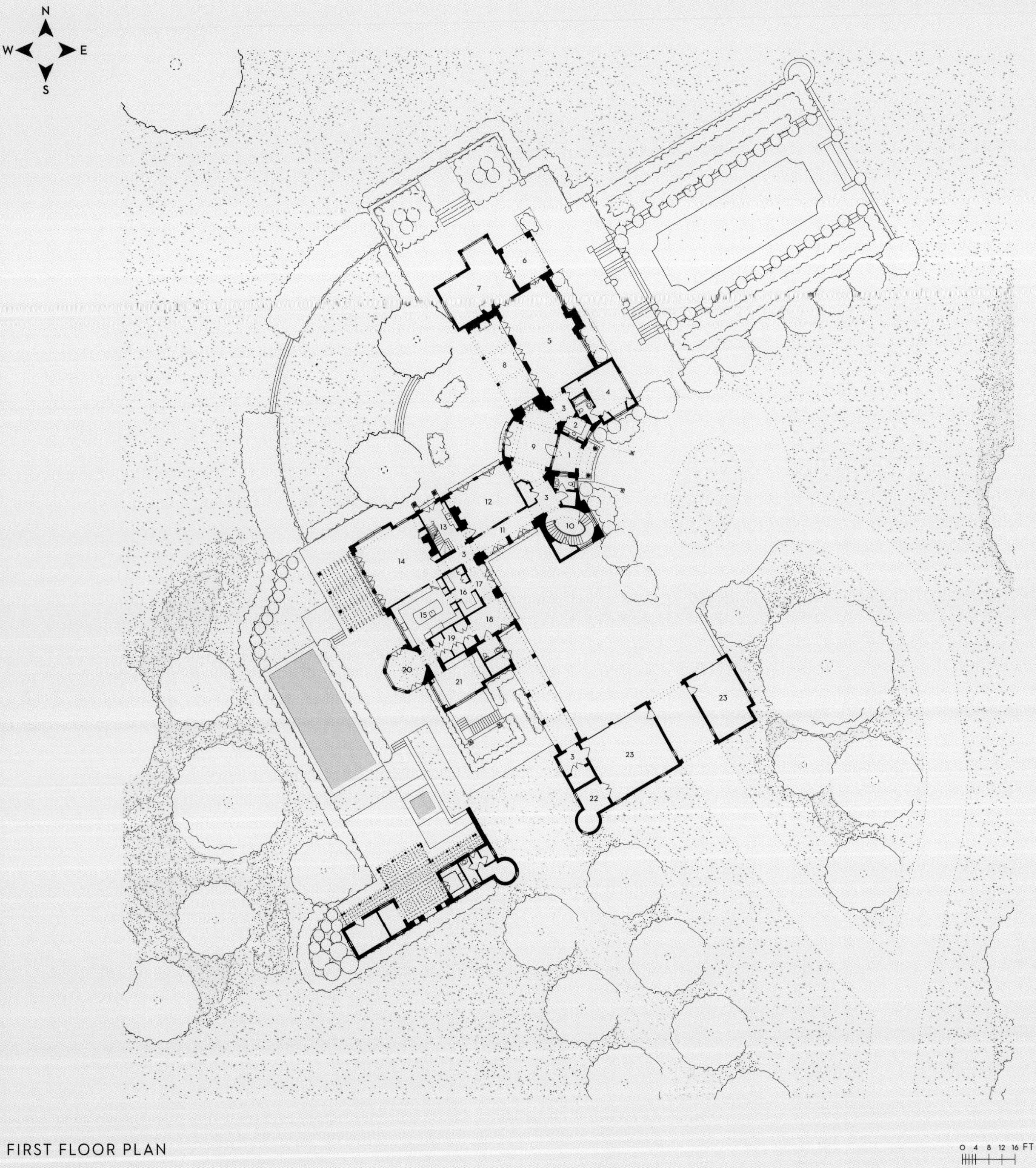

FIRST FLOOR PLAN

1. ENTRY PORCH
2. BAR
3. VESTIBULE
4. GUEST BEDROOM
5. LIVING ROOM
6. EXTERIOR PORCH
7. LIBRARY
8. LOGGIA
9. ENTRY
10. STAIR HALL
11. GALLERY
12. DINING ROOM
13. MUDROOM STAIR
14. FAMILY ROOM
15. KITCHEN
16. PANTRY
17. HALL
18. ENTRY HALL
19. MUDROOM
20. BREAKFAST ROOM
21. CHILDREN'S ROOM
22. MECHANICAL ROOM
23. GARAGE

–

Page 211, (Elliptical Stair), The elliptical stair was a collaboration between the architect and two friends, a talented stair builder and gifted ironworker.

Spread 212-213, (Aerial), The most fundamental relationship of our home, visible clearly from above, is between the formal drive and the house's culmination, an arced terrace and lawn overlooking the sound and the sunset.

Opposite, (Garden). A walled garden designed with landscape architect, Peter Cummin, is a wonderful place for a party.

This Page, (Towers). While the driveway was redirected off the allée, two towers still greet the parallel lines of trees.

–

(Front Hall), The view across the harbor is the first thing to greet a visitor to the home.

–

(Dining Room), The dining room directly adjoins the front hall, and its window enjoys the same view.

–

(Living Room), A paneled wall frames the fireplace in the living room.

–

(Daybed), Upstairs, a daughter's room is set on axis with the allée, so that her window perfectly aligns with the trees beyond.

–

(Loggia), We made a loggia outside the living room and study oriented towards the view. The window in the chimney above is onto the master bathroom.

(Outdoor Fireplace), The interior of the loggia has a fireplace, to stay warm after watching the sunset.

Project drawing, Morgen Fleisig & Rita Marks
Project photography, Durston Saylor & Tim Lee

PROCESS.

The home's front hall spans between the car drive and the terrace. The line between the two became an axis of symmetry between the dining room and living room. By working simultaneously in plan and perspective rendering we refined this crucial moment of arrival.

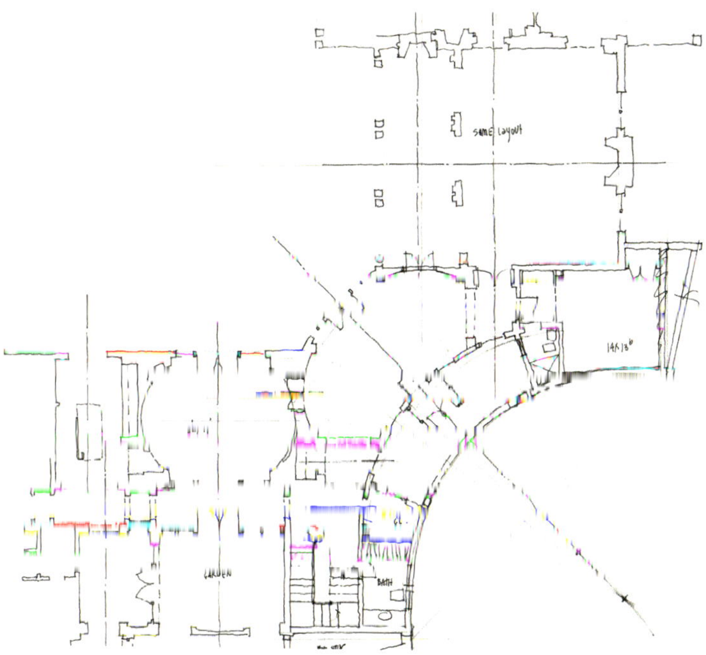

HARBOR VIEW HOUSE

SOUTHPORT
CONNECTICUT

No home is an island. To build a new home in the communities where we often work requires a close attention to site, context, history and bones. This village, a former port on the coast of Connecticut, is a New England treasure. Its hundred and fifty houses include pristine examples from every 19th century style. Together they form a neighborhood cherished by its inhabitants for the simple elegance to be found on every lot and corner.

Rather than a source of red tape and bureaucracy, we find historic districts valuable resources as repositories of local knowledge and counselors in understanding context. To wit, for this home we took our cue from John Calvin Stevens, the author of a book encountered in the bibliography of the local historic district, *American Domestic Architecture*. A Maine architect, Stevens was an able and early pioneer of that quintessentially American vernacular – one in which we often work – the Shingle Style. Named for the shingles that adorned its outside, the real key to the Shingle Style is the structure inside, the wooden 'balloon' frame. Easy to erect, modify, and capable of taking almost any shape, the balloon frame's ease and durable flexibility are at the core of what makes Shingle Style homes so good. That structure allows for deep porches, protruding bays, and dormers. It condones the easy combination of gables, towers and whimsy.

Here, that flexibility allowed us to compose a home with two beginnings. The first is the front door facing the street, the point of arrival for guests. The second is the door near the back of the house, positioned to greet those arriving by car. Each has a vestibule or mudroom, each has a stair going to the second floor, and each has a porch to shelter waiting guests as they come out of the rain. A shared vocabulary – the Doric columns that frame each door – places the two in conversation. The vestibule by the front door provides party guests easy access to the home's more formal rooms.

A mudroom on the other end catches the *je ne sais quoi* that the children often bring back with them when they arrive in the garage.

Between those two doors is the heart of the home with a family room, the kitchen, library, and a screened-in porch. The family has classical taste and modern sensibilities – that is to say they wanted the kitchen, living, and dining all to happen in the one space. A longtime collaborator with the office, the interior designer Eve Robinson, helped reconcile these sensibilities, nesting furniture groupings that made this single space do the work of four rooms. She put forth a palette of beiges, creams and blues in sympathy to tie together this room with the rest of the house and sea and sky beyond. We provided a paneled ceiling above adding scale and character to a large room without making them too heavy. In the crook of the library, porch, and kitchen, the pool and its adjoining patio are organized as their own room.

On the opposite side from the pool, in the middle of the family room, the family had one more request – a place for its Christmas tree. A simple bay window serves the purpose, providing a meeting place between the fireplaces that bookend the room.

When our family acquired this lot, a longtime field of grass close to the coast, the town showed a vigorous and understandable concern for the quality of the new home. We dug deep into local libraries and history, taking the house through a dozen iterations. We developed the design not just in the context of the needs of our family, but also the needs of their new neighbors. By working hard to understand and meet the needs of both, the design became much better. It became a place the town can proudly call neighbor, and the family can call home.

FIRST FLOOR PLAN

1. FOYER
2. STAIR HALL
3. LIVING/DINING ROOM
4. BAR
5. ENTRY HALL
6. LIBRARY
7. OFFICE
8. KITCHEN
9. SCREENED PORCH
10. VESTIBULE
11. PANTRY/LAUNDRY
12. GARAGE
13. MECHANICAL ROOM
14. PORCH
15. MUDHALL

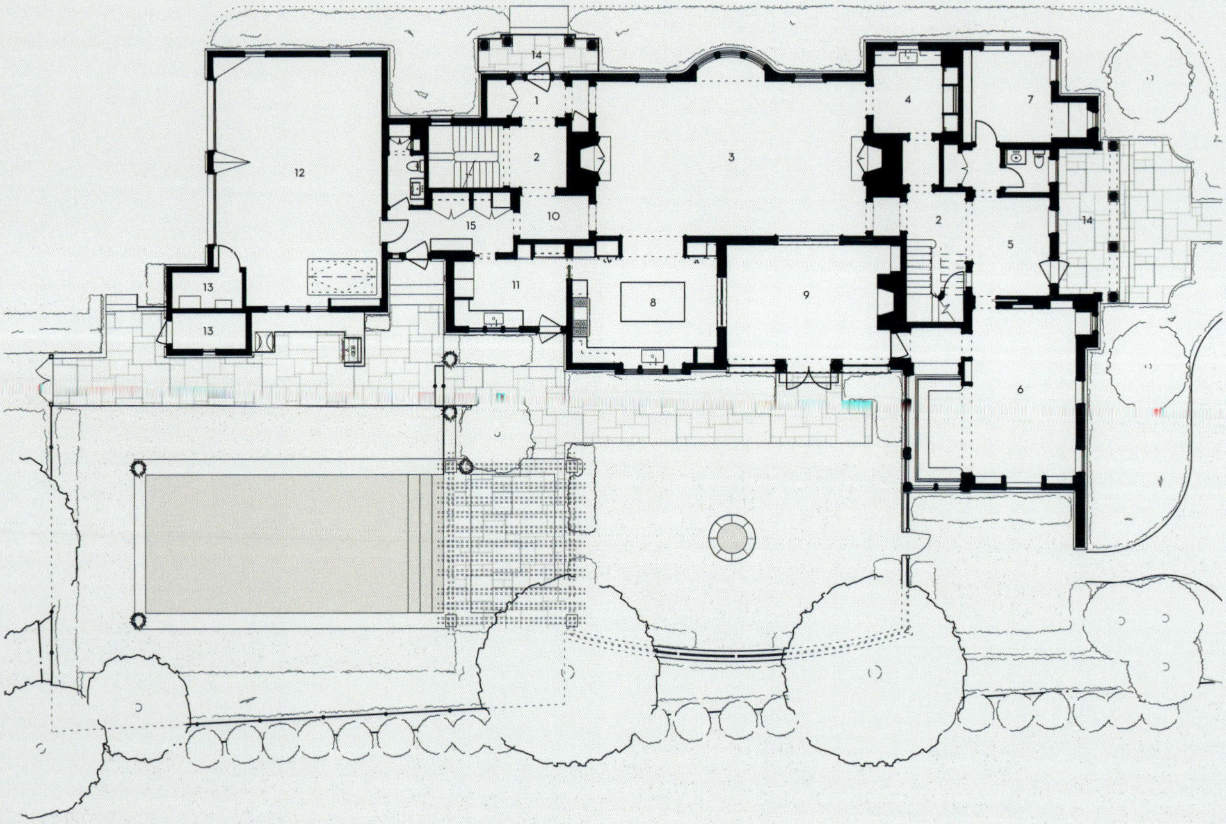

SECOND FLOOR PLAN

1. STAIR HALL
2. BEDROOM
3. MASTER BEDROOM
4. HIS BATH/DRESSING
5. HER DRESSING
6. HER BATH
7. OFFICE
8. GYM
9. COVERED PORCH

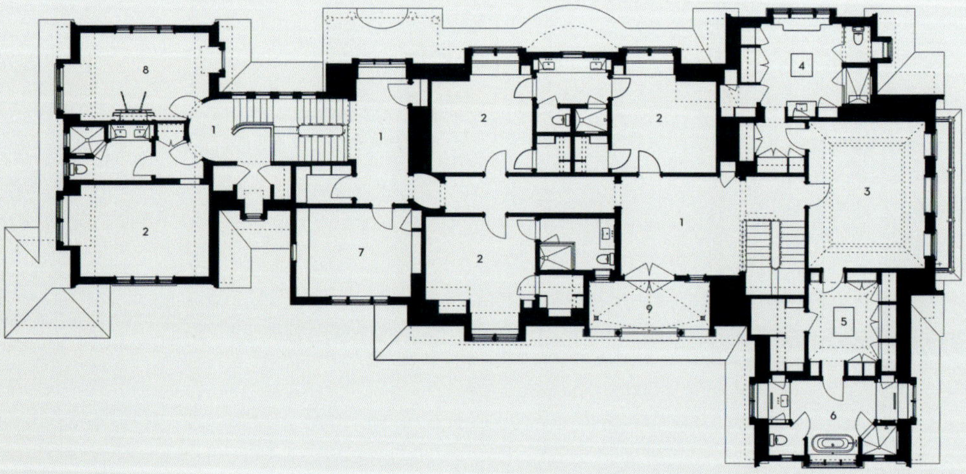

0 4 8 12 16 FT

EDWARD
WESTON
125 PHOTOGRAPHS
LAROUSSE WINE
ART

Page 227, (Front porch),
The rhythm of the front porch is echoed in the windows of the master bedroom [illegible]

Spread 228-229, (Side door),
A second porch protects visitors coming through the side entrance. To its left is a bay window, specifically requested for the Christmas tree.

This Spread (Library), From its mahogany paneling to its mustard yellow Ottoman, the library offers a space for reading and playing cards.

–

(Landing), The stair landing is a space of its own with French doors leading to a second storey porch with harbor views.

—

(Stairs). The elliptical arches at the landings echo those of the front porch.

–

(Pool), In the crook of the library, porch, and kitchen, the pool and its adjoining patio are organized as an outdoor room.

–

(Living Room), The family wanted the kitchen, living, and dining to be open – a few subtle partitions and nested furniture groupings allowed this single space to do the work of four rooms.

(Screened Porch). Anchored by a random ashlar fireplace and nested between the living room and pool, the family reports this porch to be their favorite space.

Project drawing, Olivia Rowan
Project photography, Durston Saylor

WATCH HILL HOUSE

WATCH HILL
RHODE ISLAND

A home is rarely really finished. There is always room for improvement or adjustment. Such changes are best decided upon, however, through time – through living – through experience. Few communities understand that better than the New England summer town, Watch Hill. *The New York Times* once noted how this beachside haven – Rhode Island's quieter, more family oriented counterpart to the glamor and glitz of Newport – is characterized by its, "privacy-loving, multigenerational families tucked into century-old shingled houses," many of them lived in by families for several generations. From that perspective, our family – who had lived in their shingle house for fifteen years – were relative newcomers. It was natural that, a decade gone by, they had found some improvements to be made.

Though the house stands but a stone's toss from the Rhode Island coast, the family was acutely aware that the home's plan left the life of the family cut off from its view out across the ocean. Though an open porch greeted this view, and it was framed dynamically off a back corner, a stiff set of seldom-used formal rooms monopolized access to this porch and corner, chopping them off from the rest of the house. Though the view was at the back, the real life of the home was in the family room and kitchen at the front. An octagonal dining room sat off to the side. Small windows compounded the matter. The only part of the house that was working was that back porch, fully open to the ocean, which everyone loved.

As homes improve over time, so too does design improve when the collaboration between the client and the architect extends across multiple projects. Indeed, most of our clients have returned to us for multiple projects. This project was our second with this family, so we both understood their tastes and they trusted our abilities. Frank conversations, subtle adjustments and sensitive strategic tweaks slowly led to bolder measures. When the initial demolition work revealed decay,

the project became a complete gut renovation. The rearrangement of a few closets and removal of a few walls converted the formal rooms into one flowing living and dining area. It culminated in that corner, which – with new French doors and floor-to-ceiling windows – opened the house onto the porch. The kitchen was moved entirely so that it could operate from front to back and be more connected to the living room and porch. The determined focus on the ocean views continued to the second floor, where a new window expands a bedroom's view out, and a screened in sleeping porch provides the family a place to wake up to the ocean.

Eve Robinson helped arrive at a set of finishes and furnishings equal to the improved plan. Blue is the predominant color, natural materials and colors are throughout, and attention was given to preserve the parts of the house worth preserving, such as a handsome, nautically inspired, wood-lined study tucked in a gable.

Change may be inevitable – a house may never be finished – but when we embark on any project, we work to make sure all foreseeable needs are met. As Eisenhower quipped, "plans are worthless, but planning is everything." Other needs may inevitably arise in the future, but today's needs will be answered. Though most of the exterior of the house would remain the same, we ripped out and replaced much of the interior. Heating, cooling, finishes and structure were all given the attention they needed to leave the family with a home that will serve them well for generations to come. Structure was bolstered, leaving them with a frame ready for the winds, waves, and even occasional hurricanes of the Rhode Island coast. And though we renovated with the long term in mind, our schedule was in fact very constrained. So that the family would not miss a summer, the whole project lasted just eight months.

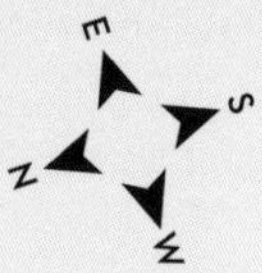

EXISTING FIRST FLOOR PLAN

1. ENTRY
2. HALL
3. LIVING ROOM
4. FAMILY ROOM
5. DINING ROOM
6. BREAKFAST
7. KITCHEN
8. PANTRY
9. BUTLER'S PANTRY
10. PLAYROOM
11. LAUNDRY
12. SCREENED PORCH
13. COVERED PORCH

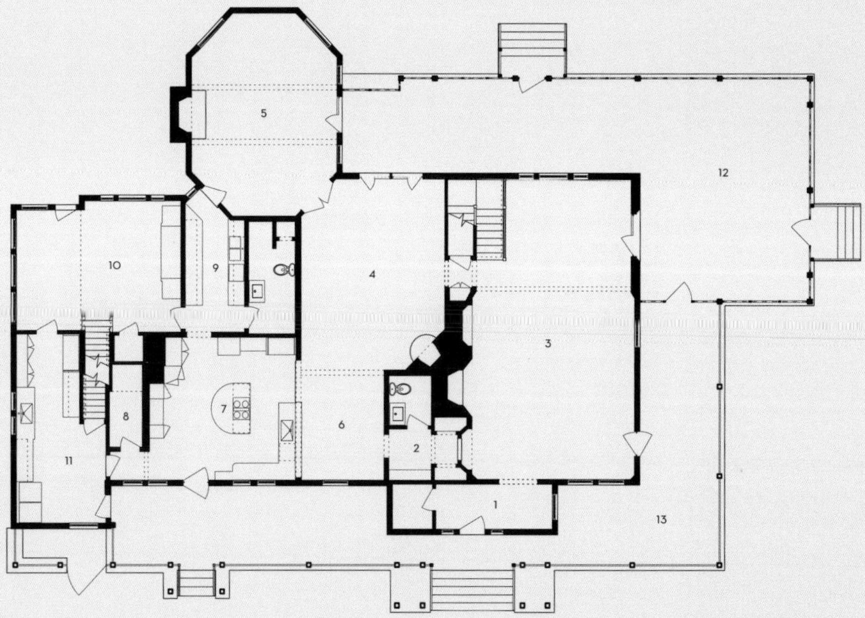

COMPLETED FIRST FLOOR PLAN

1. ENTRY
2. LIVING ROOM
3. DINING ROOM
4. BREAKFAST
5. KITCHEN
6. SITTING ROOM
7. PANTRY
8. MUDHALL
9. LAUNDRY
10. TV/PLAYROOM
11. SCREENED PORCH
12. COVERED PORCH

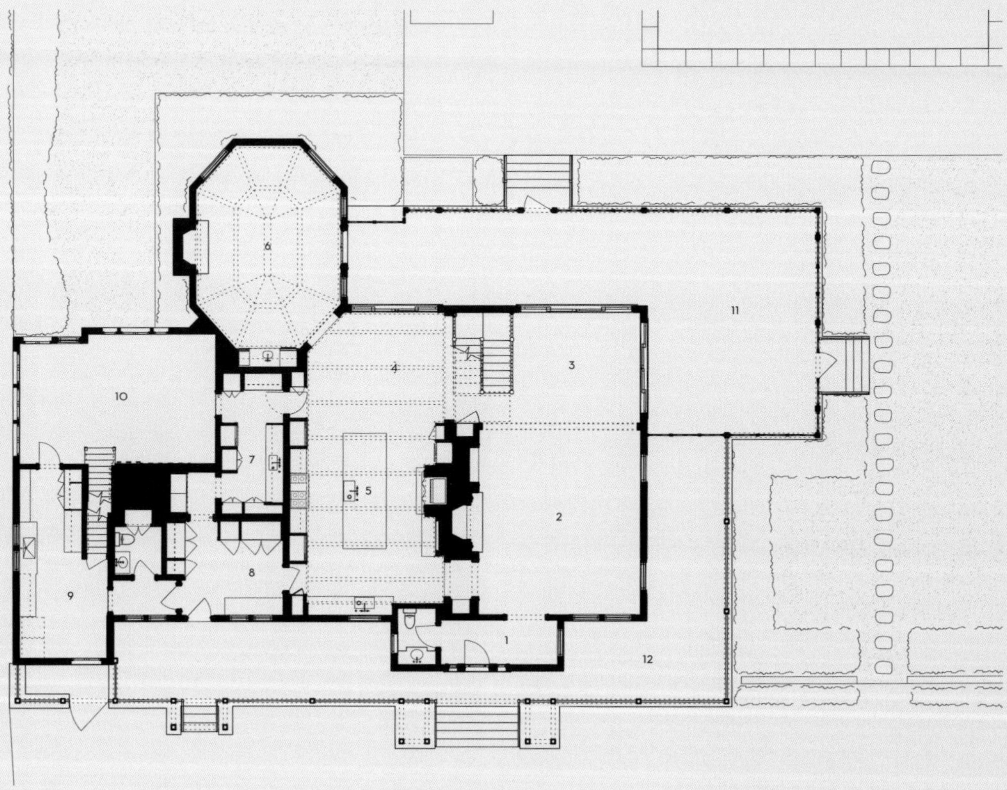

–

Spread 242-243 (Exterior), Many Watch Hill families have been in their homes for generations. Our family – who had lived in their shingle house for fifteen years – were relative newcomers.

Opposite (Kitchen), The kitchen was moved entirely so that it could flow from front to back and be more connected to the living room and porch.

This Page (Living Room), We reimagined the living room, formerly isolated from other spaces, by opening the room to adjacent spaces and views.

—

(Living Room), In the corner, new French doors and floor-to-ceiling windows opened the house onto the porch.

–

(Stair), We freed the stair to better connect the living room and kitchen.

–

(Porch), The home culminates in a screened porch, with views to the sea beyond.

–

Project drawing, Olivia Rowan
Project photography, Peter Margonelli

BEACH HOUSE

QUOGUE
LONG ISLAND

This home, on a Long Island beachfront, began with an opportunity and a constraint. The client's property came with a dilapidated little house with sweeping views to sea and east and west along the dunes. It was built, however, well seaward of where regulations allow new construction. If torn down, it could not be rebuilt in the same place. If renovated, it could only be expanded modestly, and elevated on pilings to protect against flooding. Our clients and their children, however, wanted a spacious home to entertain their extended family and friends. But they did not want to surrender their little house and its views. Rather than surrender the house and its position, we worked with the regulatory authorities and the neighbors to reduce the size of the existing dwelling, elevate it on pilings to mitigate the flood hazard, and even adjust it slightly to improve the neighbor's views. The leftover square footage became an elevated bridge. This bridge connected to the main living spaces of the house, constructed as a separate but linked pavilion.

The project thus became both a renovation and a much larger addition. The little house provided intimate proportions for an aerie of private rooms, including the master bedroom and adjacent study. The larger spaces, including kitchen, dining room, living room, screened porch and decks are in the pavilion positioned landward of the regulated line. They are all on the second floor, so as to maximize how far they can see. Indeed, the angle of the bridge, living room, kitchen and aerie is such that their views extend across and over the dunes.

This house has a destination – the sea – and the roofs all open towards it obligingly. The family wanted inside and out to flow together, so doors are everywhere. There are twenty ways into and out of the house. Working with our longtime partner landscape architect Ed Hollander, we planned a garden to wrap the home's boardwalk. He selected mainly native plants that would thrive on the challenge of winds and salt spray.

A geothermal system and solar panels minimize the home's energy impact.

In its details and style, the house is modern. Now there are some who would lump together every style under the banner 'Traditional,' name it the born nemesis of 'Modern,' or 'Modernism,' and declare heated and endless war between them. These squabbles have never made much sense to us. Modernism is one of many approaches to building, with its own strengths and insights to offer.

Born in the first blush of a newly industrial and electrified society, a world marveling at the car, the plane, and steel, Modernism was perhaps best characterized by the architectural historian Nikolaus Pevsner. In his 1936 book, *The Pioneers of Modern Design,* he identified Modernism's driving criteria as humility – that is, the building should be quiet, a frame to glorify, as he puts it dramatically, "the creative energy of this world in which we live and work."

From our practical perspective, such an approach means surfaces that get out of the way. The windows are expansive, and the finishes quiet. Modern does not though mean there are no details, no ornament – if anything those places where mechanical systems surface, or parts come together, require even more attention when there are no columns or moldings to pull upon. Interior designer Eve Robinson played a key role here, defining a color and material palette of warm and sandy tones to pull the sun and dunes into the home. The home becomes a frame for objects made well, be they the propeller-like Boffi fans, or the hand-blown glass chandeliers, perched above the dining table. Even the stairs work as a piece of art, their dual stringers and slender supports in blackened steel floating in a windowed double-height tower. All this effort is to make a home that feels, in effect, quite casual and at ease, one in harmony with its surroundings, its art, and its family.

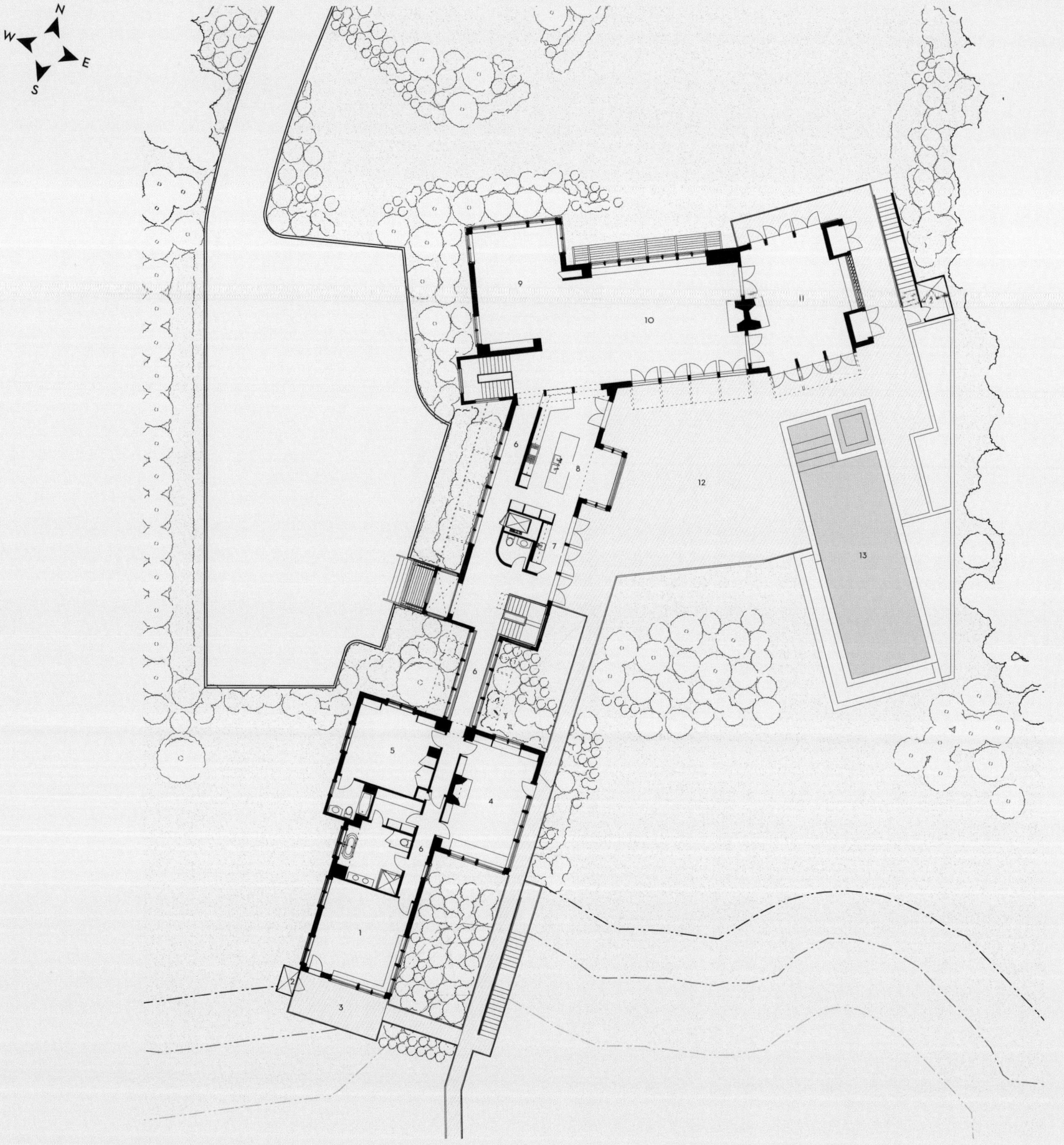

MAIN FLOOR PLAN

1. MASTER BEDROOM
2. OUTDOOR SHOWER
3. PRIVATE DECK
4. DEN
5. BEDROOM
6. HALL
7. PANTRY
8. KITCHEN
9. DINING ROOM
10. LIVING ROOM
11. SCREENED PORCH
12. DECK
13. POOL

–

Page 253, (Bridge),
By placing all the main rooms on the second floor, we elevated them above the sand dunes, permitting direct access to the beach beyond.

Spread 254-255, (Pool),
The pool mirrors the angle of the aerie.

Opposite, (Stairs),
The stairs work as a piece of art, their dual stringers and slender supports in blackened stainless steel floating in a windowed double-height tower.

This Page, (Dining Room),
The home becomes a frame for objects made well, such as these hand-blown glass chandeliers, suspended above the dining table.

–

(Living Room),
The living room's chimney stone, pale oak floors, and fabrics complement one another and bring in the color of the sand.

(Porch), The screened porch has views across the dune from bay to ocean and the louvered windbreak allows the bay view while creating shelter.

–

(Study), The master study enjoys a commanding view of the sea.

–

(Master Bedroom), The master bedroom positioned closest to the sea and dune commands an unparalleled view.

(Master Bath), Cerused oak, dolomiti marble and a sputnik chandelier create a serene bath.

Next Spread (Evening), View of the home from the beach, on a summer evening.

Project drawing, John Mason
Project photography, Durston Saylor

C R A F T

Understanding Process

When Oliver Cope Architect approaches a project, we approach it with our builders and craftspeople in mind. That is, design is tempered not just by the needs of the clients and considerations of context, but also by the possibilities of craft. That means when we specify product, it is never simply a matter of what, but who, and how. When we collaborate with craftsmen, we take the time to understand how they work, and then work to push what is possible. We ask the 'stupid questions,' bringing a creative obstinance to the field, one that focuses on the process to better perfect the outcome.

F. Scott Fitzgerald famously quipped the test of a first-rate intelligence is the "ability to hold two opposed ideas in the mind at the same time, and still retain the ability to function" – good design, too, must constantly reconcile opposed ideas through building. By understanding precisely what our builders do, we find we can, together, overcome contradictions, and do more. Whether it be a gate latch or a sculptural steel and glass stair, the results are details and execution that are as unique and special as the homes they help realize.

Each of our homes represents a response to its setting, history, and the needs of its owner. Each of our homes also represents the work of a cohort that extends far beyond our office. Our architects visit their sites often, where there will on any day be a crew of five, forty, or more at work. While developing projects we will tap on longstanding relationships with craftspeople and suppliers across the world. Our team – off and on the site – will include ironworkers, marble quarrymen, hardware manufacturers, plasterers, metalworkers, window and door builders, masons, plumbers, electricians, carpenters, and the construction crew on site, putting it all together.

To demonstrate the depth of craft that runs between all of our homes, here we have gathered some glimpses into a few of the shops of our many collaborators. Oliver Cope Architect is proud to have worked with many of these craftsmen through multiple projects and across the years, sometimes even decades.

IRON

Photography: Ken Eddy

(Top) A worker heats wrought iron in a forge in the workshop of Spirit Ironworks. Iron needs to be brought to 1,400 to 2,300 degrees, depending on whether it will be bent, thinned, thickened, punched or welded. The wheel of a hundred-ton friction screw press is on his left. *(Bottom Left)* Tim Miller, who with his sister Rachel owns and operates Spirit Ironworks, inspects a forging at his workstation to check for shape and texture. *(Bottom Right)* A worker shapes wrought iron on a 500-pound power hammer. The power hammer is over a century old and was restored to working order by the shop. It is operated by a foot pedal that controls the hammer's action. Power comes through a spinning leather belt.

BRASS

The term for hand hammering a piece of hardware, be it in steel, bronze, or brass, is peening, a technique first pioneered in Germany in the 1920s. It is one of the steps which elevates the custom-made hardware we seek out for our homes above the rest. Here Brian L. peens a doorknob using a custom-made punch at Classic Brass, a family owned firm in Jamestown, New York. Says Chris Creighton, the owner, "When you hammer a piece, and give it a polished nickel finish, it truly takes on the appearance of being jewelry."

GLASS

The skills involved with crafting stained glass extend straight back to the Middle Ages. Rosalind Brenner, founder of Manor Art Glass, cuts her glass with an oiled diamond tipped wheel on a wooden handle, similar to the tools with which her predecessors cut glass at Chartres Cathedral. Lengths of H channel lead 'came' are cut to size and fitted around the glass pieces. Then she solders each joint and seals came to glass with linseed oil putty. Here she and her partner, Michael Cardacino, stand in their East Hampton workshop behind part of an artisan lay light for one of our homes. The opalescent glass is combined with a beveled clear glass border and centerpieces that act like prisms, to refract light throughout the front stair foyer.

STONE

Shadows depict depth in working drawings, above. Craftspeople translate that depth into the third dimension through carving, through subtraction. On the top left, a carver at the British firm Chesneys uses a dummy mallet and carving chisel to restore an 18th century mantelpiece. Chisels, files, calipers, and a compass divider all lay nearby. On bottom left is a limestone balustrade detail at one of our homes. The limestone was quarried in Indiana and cut and hand carved in Englewood Cut Stone's shop located near the quarry

WOOD

Joe Grace *(top)* makes stiles for cabinet doors from poplar wood. He is a partner at Nordic Custom Builders and is in their Westchester workshop, which they have had now for 17 years. Their homes in and around New York and Connecticut are distinguished by their execution of detail, such as *(bottom right)* corbel brackets for one of our homes in the Hamptons to form the underside of a soffit, or *(bottom left)* profile knives, each ready to resolve a particular corner or molding.

M A R B L E

The chief considerations when using marble are source, cut, craft, and application. Consider the creation of a marble stair in a Park Avenue apartment we designed. Marble is metamorphic, its qualities deriving from events of immense heat and pressure, and therefore bears the imprint of its origin — on the left a quarry in Vila Viçosa in Évora, Portugal. Its proper use starts at the quarry, because the slab's cut determines its color, grain, and direction. In Marble Crafters workshop in Trainer, Pennsylvania, this ancient material is handled with advanced machines, such as a diamond abrasive high-pressure water jet, and gentle care, such as this stone craftsman *(top right)* using a Dremel tool to distress the stone's edges. Finally, with the proper frame and miter *(middle right)* the piece — only ¾" thick — comes together to achieve the effect, in the words of Bob Capoferri, the founder of Marble Crafters, "as though it was still a part of the quarry wall."

ON SITE

Our architects visit their sites often, where there will on any day be a crew of five, forty, or more at work. Here are some scenes from those sites, ranging from a crew raising a barn, to celebrating the topping off of a tower. As we develop our designs, draft our drawings, and resolve our details, we are always thinking of these crews, and how to make the best use of their work.

IN THE SHOP

Our passion for understanding the details of building starts with the boss. Oliver Cope spends his weekends in his shop. It is a habit that began with his father, a lawyer, who would always organize family projects. Weekend and summer life revolved around erecting a new garage, building stone walls, fixing plumbing. It is what they did for fun. It is still what Oliver does for fun.

SELECTED WORKS

How do you make a home that is both at peace with its past, and ready for the future?

These questions have had our attention since Oliver's first house, the Rhode Island Shingle (1985). Its outbuildings form a forecourt and exterior 'room,' creating a sum larger than its parts. In another early project, the Martha's Vineyard Tiny House (1991), he made the best of a small budget and a great site by stretching the first floor height to make the house lightheartedly grand while securing the bedroom above views of the ocean.

The same considerations for the site and the future were on our mind in the masterplan for Friends Academy (1995) in Locust Valley. Over time the school realized our design and replaced a cluttered center with a quadrangle defined by our new library and commons, the latter graced by an arched portal to greet pick-up and drop-off.

Working with context often means working with local history. After completing a farmhouse in Ligonier, PA (1996) for a young family, they later asked us to design a "constellation" of barns (2015), leading us to honor the Pennsylvania Forebay Bank Barn. Working with context can also mean working within a tradition, in this case a team of itinerant timber framers and barn raisers. Our clients' little girls grew up and there have been two weddings in the new bank barn.

We enjoy learning from predecessors, such as Harrie T. Lindeberg, Polhemus & Coffin and others through renovations and alterations of their work. In a renovation in Matinecock on Long Island's North Shore (2016), we found ways to enhance and build upon the work of Bradley Delehanty, who had slipped an Art Deco ocean liner into a white brick Georgian – literally. He detailed a double height library with elements salvaged from the RMS *Mauretania*. We matched his style in a new jewel box-like bar and his restraint in a serene kitchen and conservatory breakfast room.

We do not see a distinction between renovations and new homes. Whether a family begins with a forest (p.54), a small beach shack (p.250), or a Delano & Aldrich estate (p.84), a truly good home improves over time, as each generation makes its own considered contribution. Over the past thirty years, it has brought us great joy to help successive generations craft homes where families gather and make memories together.

Rhode Island Shingle

Location: Rhode Island
Year: 1985
Project Architect: Oliver Cope
Contractor: M.F. Smith Associates

Astor Court Apartment

Location: Manhattan, New York
Year: 1990
Project Architect: Oliver Cope

Centre Island Guest House

Location: Centre Island
Year: 1990
Project Architect: Olivia Rowan
Interior Designer: David Easton
Contractor: Sherf & Hacker

New Centre Island Estate

Location: Centre Island, New York
Year: 1990
Project Architects: Olivia Rowan & Oliver Cope
Project Team: John Pelligra, Robert C. Wilkanowski
Interior Designer: David Easton
Construction Manager: Peter Talty

Martha's Vineyard Tiny House

Location: Martha's Vineyard, Massachusetts
Year: 1991
Project Architect: Oliver Cope
Contractor: Bird Brown Company

Greenwich House

Location: Greenwich, Connecticut
Year: 1993
Project Architect: Olivia Rowan
Project Team: Robert Willis
Contractor: Burke & Matthews

Upper West Side Townhouse (p.180-183)

Location: Manhattan, New York
Year: 1994
Project Architect: Thomas W. Gay
Interior Designer: Victoria Hagen
Contractor: SMI Construction Management

Riverside House

Location: Riverside, Connecticut
Year: 1994
Project Architect: Rita Marks
Project Team: Morgen Fleisig

Stonington Residence

Location: Stonington, Connecticut
Year: 1995
Project Architect: Olivia Rowan
Project Team: Morgen Fleisig
Contractor: Blackstone Construction

Master Plan and design for quadrangle, library and the commons and Performing Arts Center at Friends Academy

Location: Locust Valley, New York
Year: 1995, *Built*
Project Architect: Oliver Cope
Project Team: Morgen Fleisig

Park Avenue Apartment

Location: Manhattan, New York
Year: 1996
Project Architect: Olivia Rowan
Interior Designer: Robert Couturier
Contractor: SMI Construction Management

Townhouse

Location: Manhattan, New York
Year: 1996
Project Architect: Joanna Frank
Contractor: SMI Construction Management

Rye House Renovation & Addition

Location: Rye, New York
Year: 1996
Project Architect: Joanna Frank
Landscape Architect: Cummin Associates
Contractor: Mason & Krabbe

Stahlstown House

Location: Pennsylvania
Year: 1997
Project Architect: Rita Marks
Project Team: Olivia Rowan & Morgen Fleisig
Interior Designer: Navarro Design Associates

Greenwich House

Location: Greenwich, Connecticut
Year: 1997
Project Architect: Olivia Rowan
Project Team: Rita Marks & Morgen Fleisig
Interior Designer: MAC II (Mica Ertegun)

Norman House (p.208-223)

Location: Centre Island, New York
Year: 1997
Project Architect: Oliver Cope
Project Team: Morgen Fleisig & Anthony Minichetti
Interior Designer: Sherill Canet Interiors
Contractor: Mayfair Construction

Greenwich Renovation

Location: Greenwich, Connecticut
Year: 1998
Project Architect: Joanna Frank
Contractor: Nordic Custom Builders

Italianate House

Location: Centre Island, New York
Year: 1998
Project Architect: Oliver Cope
Project Team: Grainne Cassidy, Jenny Smith, Morgen Fleisig
Contractor: Qualico Construction

Scarsdale Renovation

Location: Scarsdale, New York
Year: 1998
Project Architect: Oliver Cope
Interior Designer: Ingrao Design
Contractor: Nordic Custom Builders

Old Westbury House

Location: Old Westbury, New York
Year: 1999
Project Architect: Olivia Rowan
Interior Designer: Sherrill Canet Interiors
Landscape Architect: Hollander Design
Contractor: Qualico Construction

Fishers Island House

Location: Fishers Island, New York
Year: 1999
Project Architect: Morgen Fleisig
Contractor: Tom Shillo, Z&S Construction

Shingle House (p.194-207)

Location: Cove Neck, New York
Year: 2001
Project Architect: Olivia Rowan
Project Team: Morgen Fleisig, Grainne Cassidy, Margie Lavender, Robert Farrell
Interior Designer: Simek Howard
Landscape Architect: Cummin Associates
Contractor: Mayfair Construction

Butterfly House (p.54-67)

Location: Muttontown, New York
Year: 2002
Project Architect: Oliver Cope
Project Team: Jim Harwood
Contractor: Owner

Scarsdale Renovation

Location: Scardale, New York
Year: 2002
Project Architect: Oliver Cope
Project Team: Jairo Castro
Interior Designer: Michelle Gerson Interiors
Contractor: Taconic Builders

Long Island House

Location: Coveneck, New York
Year: 2003
Project Architect: Oliver Cope
Project Team: Jim Harwood
Contractor: Mayfair Construction

Country Estate (p.68-83)

Location: Old Westbury, New York
Year: 2003
Project Architect: Olivia Rowan
Project Team: Morgen Fleisig, Jairo Castro, Joyce Wang, Robert Farrell
Interior Designer: Sherrill Canet Interiors
Landscape Architect: Hollander Design
Contractor: Qualico Contracting

Upper West Side Townhouse (p.180-183)

Location: Manhattan, New York
Year: 2003
Project Architect: Oliver Cope
Project Team: Jim Harwood
Contractor: Nordic Custom Builders

Country Estate Guest House (p.68-83)

Location: Old Westbury, New York
Year: 2003
Project Architect: Jairo Castro
Contrator: Qualico Construction

Stonington Renovation

Location: Stonington, Connecticut
Year: 2004
Project Architect: Morgen Fleisig & Piotr Redlinksi
Interior Designer: Brian J. McCarthy
Landscape Architect: Cummin Associates
Contrator: Wolman Construction

Laurel Hollow Renovation

Location: Laurel Hollow, New York
Year: 2005
Project Architect: Oliver Cope
Contrator: Owner

West End Apartment

Location: Manhattan, New York
Year: 2005
Project Architect: Margie Lavender
Interior Designer: Nancy Galasso Interiors
Contractor: Nordic Custom Builders

Lenox Hill Townhouse (p.176-179)

Location: Manhattan, New York
Year: 2005
Project Architect: Rita Marks
Project Team: Jairo Castro
Interior Designer: Michael Batterbee & Associates
Contractor: Eurostruct

Carnegie Hill Apartment

Location: Manhattan, New York
Year: 2006
Project Architect: Olivia Rowan
Project Team: Elizabeth Benko
Contractor: Nordic Custom Builders

Beach House (p.250-265)

Location: Quogue, New York
Year: 2006
Project Architect: Olivia Rowan
Project Team: Morgen Fleisig, U-Jin Choi, Euisik Hong
Interior Designer: Eve Robinson Associates
Contractor: SMI Construction Management

East River Duplex (p.102-115)

Location: Manhattan, New York
Year: 2007
Project Architect: Rita Marks
Project Team: Alfonso Langone & Tricia Rizzi
Interior Designer: Ingrao Design
Contractor: DiSalvo Contracting

Lenox Hill Townhouse

Location: Manhattan, New York
Year: 2008
Project Architect: Rita Marks
Project Team: Todd Iannantuono
Contractor: McCormack Contracting

Oyster Bay Estate

Location: Oyster Bay, New York
Year: 2008
Project Architect: Alison Guneyik
Project Team: Todd Iannantuono,
Rita Marks, Joyce Wang
Interior Designer: Tham Kannalikham
Contractor: Mayfair Construction,
Nordic Custom Builders

Oyster Bay Poolhouse

Location: Oyster Bay, New York
Year: 2008
Project Architect: Margie Lavender & Jairo Castro
Contractor: Mayfair Construction

North Haven House

Location: North Haven, New York
Year: 2009
Project Architect: Oliver Cope
Project Team: Kenneth Wiland
Interior Designer: Joanne DePalma
Contractor: Mayfair Construction

Reimagining Delano & Aldrich (p.84-99)

Location: Old Westbury, New York
Year: 2009
Project Architect: Olivia Rowan
Project Team: Joyce Wang
Interior Designer: S.R. Gambrel
Landscape Architect: Innocenti & Webel
Contractor: SMI Construction Management

Carnegie Hill Townhouse (p.184-187)

Location: Manhattan, New York
Year: 2010:
Project Architect: Rita Marks
Project Team: Euisik Hong
Interior Designer: Pamplemousse Design
Contractor: SMI Construction Management

Old Westbury Stone House (p.26-39)

Location: Old Westbury, New York
Year: 2010
Project Architect: Rita Marks
Project Team: Todd Iannantuono & Alfonso Langone
Interior Designer: Cullman & Kravis Associates
Contractor: Owner

Oxford Road Renovation

Location: Scarsdale, New York
Year: 2010
Project Architect: Jairo Castro
Contractor: Nordic Custom Builders

Palm Beach Renovation

Location: Palm Beach, Florida
Year: 2010
Project Architect: Oliver Cope
Project Team: Catherine Kirchhoff
Interior Designer: Lars Bolander
Landscape Architect: Mario Nievera Design
Contractor: Benitz Building

Harbor View House (p.224-237)

Location: Southport, Connecticut
Year: 2011
Project Architect: Olivia Rowan
Project Team: Joyce Wang,
Kate Fixmer, Todd Iannantuono
Interior Designer: Eve Robinson Associates
Landscape Architect: Cummin Associates
Contractor: Mayfair Construction

Adirondack House (p.40-53)

Location: North Elba, New York
Year: 2011
Project Architect: Olivia Rowan
Project Team: Rita Marks & Jairo Castro
Contractor: R.P. Ledger Construction

Oyster Bay Bridge

Location: Oyster Bay, New York
Year: 2011
Project Architect: Jairo Castro
Contractor: Fuschetto & Son

Central Park Duplex (p.116-129)

Location: Manhattan, New York
Year: 2012:
Project Architect: Rita Marks
Project Team: Reidin Corbet & Emma Kelly
Interior Designer: Eve Robinson Associates
Contractor: SMI Construction Management

Carnegie Hill Apartment

Location: Manhattan, New York
Year: 2012::
Project Architect: Olivia Rowan
Project Team: Joyce Wang
Contractor: Nordic Custom Builders

Lenox Hill Apartment

Location: Manhattan, New York
Year: 2012::
Project Architect: Olivia Rowan
Project Team: Joyce Wang, Kenneth Wiland
Interior Designer: Joanne DePalma
Contractor: Nordic Custom Builders

Upper West Side Combination (p.188-191)

Location: Manhattan, New York
Year: 2012:
Project Architect: Rita Marks
Project Team: Alfonso Langone & Eusik Hong
Interior Designer: Willey Design
Contractor: SMI Construction Management

West End Avenue Aerie (p.130-143)

Location: Manhattan, New York
Year: 2013:
Project Architect: Rita Marks
Project Team: Reidin Corbet
Interior Designer: Bunny Williams
Contractor: Nordic Custom Builders

Watch Hill House (p.238-249)

Location: Watch Hill, Rhode Island
Year: 2013
Project Architect: Olivia Rowan
Project Team: Joyce Wang
Interior Designer: Eve Robinson Associates
Contractor: Gardner Woodwrights

Hampton Summer House

Location: East Hampton, New York
Year: 2013
Project Architects: Sara Statile & Todd Iannantuono
Project Team: Joyce Wang
Interior Designer: Ingrao Design
Landscape Architect: Hollander Design
Contractor: Mayfair Construction

Southampton Renovation

Location: Southampton, New York
Year: 2013
Project Architect: Olivia Rowan
Interior Designer: Ingrao Design
Contractor: Bulgin & Associates

Upper West Side Apartment

Location: Manhattan, New York
Year: 2014
Project Architect: Rita Marks
Project Team: Reidin Corbet
Interior Designer: Sara Story Design
Contractor: Nordic Custom Builders

Fifth Avenue Apartment

Location: Manhattan, New York
Year: 2014
Project Architect: Lenore Passavanti
Interior Designer: Eric Cohler Design
Contractor: Hobbs, Inc.

Glen Cove Renovation

Location: Glen Cove, New York
Year: 2014
Project Architect: Todd Iannantuono
Interior Designer: Bilhuber & Associates
Contractor: Al Gherlone, Qualico Construction

Penthouse Apartment (p.144-157)

Location: Manhattan, New York
Year: 2015
Project Architect: Jairo Castro & Syreeta Brooks
Interior Designer: Jenny Fischbach Design
Contractor: SMI Construction Management

Stahlstown Barns

Location: Stahlstown, Pennsylvania
Year: 2015
Project Architect: Oliver Cope
Project Team: Alfonso Langone
Contractor: King Construction Company

Carnegie Hill Apartment (p.158-171)

Location: Manhattan, New York
Year: 2015
Project Architect: Olivia Rowan
Project Team: Joyce Wang
Interior Designer: Erik R. Smith
Contractor: Nordic Custom Builders

East Hampton Renovation

Location: East Hampton, New York
Year: 2015
Project Architect: Dennis Park
Interior Designer: Michael Rosenberg & Associates
Landscape Architect: Garden 26
Contractor: Mayfair Construction

Matinecock Renovation

Location: Matinecock, New York
Year: 2016
Project Architect: Robie Wood
Interior Designer: Ingrao Design
Contractor: Qualico Construction

Upper East Side Townhouse

Location: Manhattan, New York
Year: 2016
Project Architect: Syreeta Brooks
Project Team: Jairo Castro & Zoë H. Lee
Interior Designer: Jenny Fischbach Design
Contractor: Highline Construction Group

Southampton Renovation

Location: Southampton, New York
Year: 2016
Project Architect: Jairo Castro
Landscape Architect: Hollander Design
Contractor: Bulgin & Associates

Chatham Pool House

Location: Chatham, New York
Year: 2016
Project Architect: Jairo Castro
Landscape Architect: Diane Devore
Interior Designer: Shawn Henderson
Contractor: Peter Whitehead Builder & Hardwick Post and Beam

Carnegie Hill Apartment

Location: Manhattan, New York
Year: 2016
Project Architect: Syreeta Brooks
Interior Designer: Jenny Fischbach Design
Contractor: Highline Construction Group

Park Avenue Apartment

Location: Manhattan, New York
Year: 2016
Project Architect: Rita Marks
Project Team: Emma Kelly
Interior Designer: Paris Forino
Contractor: DiSalvo Contracting

East Hampton House

Location: East Hampton, New York
Year: 2020
Project Architects: Olivia Rowan & Oliver Cope
Project Team: Joyce Wang, Dennis Park, Jairo Castro
Interior Designer: Ken Fulk
Landscape Architect: Laguardia Design
Contractor: Mayfair Construction

ACKNOWLEDGMENTS

It has been a privilege to work with innumerable dedicated and inspiring partners. Key among them have been my two incomparable and multi-talented principals, Olivia Rowan and Rita Marks, and our office manager, Jon Crider, who keeps our world together and has himself, over his twenty five years with us, accumulated so much experience in architecture that he can be relied on for important insights into our projects. I would like to thank the whole team in the office: Syreeta Brooks, Jairo Castro, Alicia Gonzales, Todd Iannantuono, Leah Janover, Nicolas Kemper, Dong-uk Kim, Alfonso Langone, Elizabeth Nehrbauer, Eimear O'Brien, Dennis Park, Christian Porfido, Kimberly Taracena, Joyce Wang, Parker Wilson, and Robie Wood. In addition, I'd like to acknowledge the more than one hundred colleagues who have worked with us over our three decades in practice, including Tricia Alvez, Cecilia Barker, Elizabeth Benko, David Berridge, Jessica Boling, Harry Branch-Shaw, Grainne Cassidy, John Chester, U-Jin Choi, Annie Chow, Joseph Combs, Casey Cook, Reidin Corbet, Ariana Estrella, Robert Farrell, Asta Fivgas, Kate Fixmer, Morgen Fleisig, Amy Flynn, Kathleen Ford, David Foster, Joanna Frank, Sarah Froelich, Thomas Gay, Jim Harwood, Thomas Hetherington, Jay Hobbs, Euisik Hong, Ben Horner, Alison Hovey, Hussam Jallad, Nechama Kahn, Emma Kelly, Anna Ruth Kimbrough, Catherine Kirchhoff, Leah Kreger, Jenna Larson, Margie Lavender, Zoe H. Lee, Zoe V. Lee, Darlene Levy, Melpi Magklivera, Ian McDonald, Candace Mendez, Anthony Minichetti, Anthonius Moniaga, Michael Natali, Ella O'Sullivan, Lenore Passavanti, John Pelligra, Emily Pringle, Nandini Ramamurthi, Piotr Redlinski, Kristina Reichenbach, Venessa Restrepo, Stephen Roe, Michelle Russoniello, Jennifer Smith, Cara Statile, Peter Tomashevski, Jessica Wendover, Susan Whyte, Kenneth Wiland, Robert Wilkanowski, the late Robert Willis, and Edwin Zawadzki.

No great design happens in a vacuum, and important to the success of our designs have been our colleagues in landscape architecture, interior design, engineering, and lighting design. Among many talented landscape architects, I thank especially Peter Cummin, Ed Hollander, Diane Devore, Jim Wellington, Christopher Thorp, Katherine Hermann and Christopher LaGuardia. From the field of interior design, it has been a pleasure to work with Jenny Fischbach, Eve Robinson, Jacques Grange, Serge Barbosa, Bunny Williams, Ellie Cullman, Sherrill Canet, Victoria Hagen, Tony Ingrao, Jeffrey Bilhuber, Brian J. McCarthy, Eric Cohler, Erik Smith, Casey Pugatch, Joanne DePalma, Shawn Henderson, Pat Navarro, Kathy P. Irwin, Ken Fulk, Daryl Serrett, Tim Rossi, Meg Braff, Whitney Maehara, Nancy Burfiend, Kate Emmons, Paris Forino, Miles Redd, Sara Story, Steven Gambrel, and Tham Kannalikham. Engineering is an art as practiced by Nat Oppenheimer, Deborah McGuiness, Jim Villano, Nicholas Fair, Lauren Homer, Delbert Smith, Pete Voto, Phil Khalil, Ed Hanington, Bruce Nicoll, Bruce McCutcheon, Greg Salm, Jim MacDonald, Jim DeStefano, Robert Drechsler, Ivan Pollack, Andrew Collins, Joseph Dioguardi, Jr. Among lighting designers, I would thank Robert Leiter, David Clinard, Stephen Bernstein, Peter Romaniello, and Nathan Orsman.

A good design is nothing without great execution, and for that I am thankful for the many talented builders, suppliers, and craftsmen with whom we have worked, including Steve Mark,

Tim Ryan, Eamonn Ryan, Al Gherlone, Ed Bulgin, Jeff Gagliotti, Ken Wright, Vincent DiSalvo, Wayne Haddock, Mark Dobbin, Walter Lorenz, John Tortorella, John King, John Leone, William Costello, Jim Kim, Gary Waleko, Randy Gardner, John Donadic, Josh Wiener, Michael DiSario, Pat Ledger, Andrew Baren, Amanda Valvano, Judith Prause, Rhett Butler, Erich Theophile, Bob Capoferri, James Eaton, Marcia Wadsworth, Jonathan Tibett, James Tibett, Nanz Company, Brian Trager, Peter Manning, Wainlands, Michael Reilly, Tim Carpenter, the late Kevin Zeluck, Kern/Rockenfield, Jean Wiart, Gerry Dolezar, Steve Cozzolino, Robert Ferraroni, Thomas Finsterwald, Jeff Anschlowar, Tom Tebbens, Tom Haddock, Foster Reeve, John, Bill & Scott Bretz, Joe Grace, Christian Gudmand, Ridge Shinn, Adrian Taylor, Timothy and Rachel Miller, Declan Blackmore, Jack Whitmore, Dominick Reis, Michael Merrit, Kim Michels, and Charlie Marder. Each of these professionals are craftsmen in their own right.

Corralling all the different parties is no small job. We have been fortunate to collaborate with thoughtful owner's representatives, including Mark McBreairty, Brian Ninnis, George Constant, Tom Nelson, Jack Lowe, Tony Hume, Derrick Miniken, and Joe Hallstein.

The most important partner in any of our projects is our client. Without their inspiration, counsel, and courage to see projects through, there would be no architecture.

In making a record of our work and allowing us to share some of it with the world, we have had the good luck to work with many talented partners. There are the skilled editors, writers, and photographers who published our work. I would like to thank all of the photographers we have worked with to capture our projects, including Lena Yaremenko, Peter Margonelli, Elizabeth Haynes, Scott Morris, Chuck Choi, Nicole Franzen, Roy Englebrecht, Francesco Lagnese, Kfir Ziv, Durston Saylor, Devon Banks, Eric Piasecki, Dan Nissley, Rebecca McAlpine and Tim Lee. I would like to thank Kim Taracena and Eimear O'Brien for having prepared the presentation plans which accompany each project. I would like to thank Nicolas Kemper for his help with the text. We have had a long special relationship with John Mason. His perspectival drawings have often played a role in developing our designs, and in this book help capture their spirit. It has been a gift to work with our partners at Triglyph, and we have much to be thankful for including the eye of Dylan Thomas, the pen of Clive Aslet, and the production prowess of Kate Turner.

In particular, I would like to thank a few of the people who have been especially supportive of my work as well as sources of wise counsel, in some cases from my first foray into life as a professional. My gratitude to Dan and Alisa Doctoroff, John and Elena Brim, Ray and Dorothy Guth, Judy and B.A. King, David and Verna George, Albert and Manda Kalimian, Kevin Zeluck, Peter Talty, and Douglas Cutsogeorge is unending.

Finally, I would like to thank my family. I have been fortunate to have an extended family that enjoys being together and doing things together. It is a touchstone that makes taking risks less daunting. My parents gave me the gift of unqualified love and exhibited confidence that I would turn out all right in the end. My darling and wonderful wife, Hillary, has been my fellow traveler, navigator, counselor, editor, and unstinting supporter for more than forty years. She has made all things possible. My two best beloved daughters, Sarah and Hannah, make all things worthwhile and bring me more joy than all other things combined.

Oliver Cope

CREDITS

	Front endpapers: © Olivia Rowan
2-3	© Chuck Choi
4-5	© Durston Saylor
6-9	© Chuck Choi
11	© Hannah Schillinger
17	(top left) © Oliver Cope
17	(top right & bottom left) © Hannah Schillinger
17	(bottom right) © Chuck Choi
19	© Dylan Thomas
22	© Hannah Schillinger
24-25	© Chuck Choi
27	© Rita Marks
28-29	© Durston Saylor
31	© Durston Saylor
33-39	© Durston Saylor
41	© Olivia Rowan
42-43	© Elizabeth Haynes
45-53	© Elizabeth Haynes
55	© John Mason
56-57	© Chuck Choi
59-67	© Chuck Choi
69	© John Mason
70-71	© Chuck Choi
73-78	© Chuck Choi
80	(top & center) © Olivia Rowan
80	(bottom left) © John Mason
80	(bottom right) © Chuck Choi
81-83	© Chuck Choi
85	© John Mason
87	© Eric Piasecki
89-98	© Eric Piasecki
99	(top & center) © Rita Marks
99	(bottom left) © John Mason
100-101	© Devon Banks
103	© Rita Marks
104-105	© Scott Morris of SGM
107-113	© Scott Morris of SGM
114	(top left & bottom right) © Nicolas Kemper
114	(top right & bottom left) © Rita Marks
115	© Scott Morris of SGM
117	© Rita Marks
118-119	© Eric Piasecki
122-129	© Eric Piasecki
131	© Rita Marks
134-143	© Francesco Lagnese
145	© Jairo Castro
146-147	© Durston Saylor
149-157	© Durston Saylor
159	© Olivia Rowan
161-171	© Durston Saylor
173	© Rita Marks
176	© Nicolas Kemper
178-179	© Chuck Choi
180	© Durston Saylor
182-183	© Durston Saylor
184	© Devon Banks
186-188	© Devon Banks
190-191	© Devon Banks
192-193	© Durston Saylor
195	© Morgen Fleisig
197-201	© Chuck Choi
202	(top) © Olivia Rowan
202	(bottom) © Chuck Choi
203	(top) © Chuck Choi
203	(bottom) © Olivia Rowan
204-207	© Chuck Choi
209	© Morgen Fleisig & Rita Marks
211	© Durston Saylor
212-213	© Mayfair Construction
214-215	© Tim Lee
216-219	© Durston Saylor
220-221	© Tim Lee
223	(top) © Tim Lee
225	© Olivia Rowan
227-237	© Durston Saylor
239	© Olivia Rowan
241-249	© Peter Margonelli
251	© John Mason
253-265	© Durston Saylor
267	© Ken Eddy
268	(top) © Classic Brass
268	(bottom) © Manor Art Glass
269	(top left & top right) © Chesneys
269	(bottom) © Olivia Rowan
270	© Nordic Custom Builders
271	(left, right top & right center) © Marble Crafters
271	(right bottom) © Rebecca McAlpin
273	© Oliver Cope
275	(row one left) © Larry Babis Photography
275	(row one right) © Chuck Choi
275	(row two right & center) © Chuck Choi
275	(row two right) © Eric Roth
275	(row three right) © Chuck Choi
275	(row four right & left) © Chuck Choi

276 (row one right) © Chuck Choi
276 (row two left & right) © Chuck Choi
276 (row three left) © Roy Englebrecht
276 (row three right) © Chuck Choi
276 (row four left) © Nicolas Kemper
276 (row four center) © Tim Lee
276 (row four right) © Chuck Choi
277 (row one left) © Scott Arnel
277 (row one right) © Chuck Choi
277 (row two) © Chuck Choi
277 (row three left) © Dick Miller
277 (row three right) © Chuck Choi
277 (row four left & right) © Chuck Choi
278 (row one left) © Kfir Ziv
278 (row one right) © Chuck Choi
278 (row two left) © Chuck Choi
278 (row two right) © Durston Saylor
278 (row three) © Chuck Choi
278 (row four left) © Peter Cummin
278 (row four right) © Chuck Choi
279 (row one left) © Chuck Choi
279 (row one right) © Nicolas Kemper
279 (row two left & right) © Durston Saylor
279 (row three left) © Scott Morris
279 (row three right) © L.J. Garfield
280 (row one left) © Kenneth Wiland
280 (row one center & right) © Eric Piasecki
280 (row two left) © Devon Banks
280 (row two right) © Durston Saylor
280 (row three left) © Chuck Choi
280 (row four left) © Durston Saylor
280 (row four right) © Elizabeth Haynes
281 (row one) © Nick Dawson
281 (row two left) © Eric Piasecki
281 (row three left) © Devon Banks
281 (row three right) © Francesco Lagnese
281 (row four left) © Peter Margonelli
281 (row four right) © Lena Yaremenko
282 (row one right) © Nicole Franzen
282 (row two left) © Lenore Passavanti
282 (row three left) © Durston Saylor
282 (row three right) © John King
282 (row four left) © Durston Saylor
283 (row one center) © Durston Saylor
283 (row two left & right) © Anthony Crisafulli
283 (row three left) © Durston Saylor
283 (row three right) © Rebecca McAlpin
Back endpapers: © Hannah Schillinger

COLOPHON

First published in the United Kingdom
in 2020 by Triglyph Books.

Triglyph Books
154 Tachbrook Street, London SW1V 2NE
www.TriglyphBooks.com

ISBN 978-1-9163554-1-5

Printed and bound sustainably in Italy.

OLIVER COPE
ARCHITECT

TRIGLYPH BOOKS